BREEDING BIN LADENS

Zachary Shore

BREEDING BIN LADENS

*America, Islam,
and the Future of Europe*

THE JOHNS HOPKINS UNIVERSITY PRESS
BALTIMORE

Printed in the United States of America on acid-free paper
2 4 6 8 9 7 5 3 1

The Johns Hopkins University Press
2715 North Charles Street
Baltimore, Maryland 21218-4363
www.press.jhu.edu

Library of Congress Cataloging-in-Publication Data
Shore, Zachary.
Breeding Bin Ladens : America, Islam, and the future of
Europe / Zachary Shore.
p.   cm.
Includes bibliographical references and index.
ISBN 0-8018-8505-1 (alk. paper)
1. Muslims—Europe. 2. Islam—Europe. 3. Europe—Ethnic
relations—21st century. I. Title.
D1056.2.M87S56 2006
305.6'97094—dc22   2006007080

A catalog record for this book is available from the
British Library.

To the many European Muslims who graciously shared their experiences, opinions, and time with me

Contents

Preface

Everything seemed so hopeful. When Europeans tore down the Berlin Wall, East and West embraced. In the years that followed, Europeans steadily continued knitting a hodgepodge of peoples into an ever closer union. Social cohesion is fundamental to the European dream, but that dream has lately suffered a rude awakening. While Europe's eyes were fixed on integrating the Union's new eastern member states, they overlooked a restive group growing within the West. As in November 2005, Paris burned through two weeks of violence, Americans looked on with grim unease, and Europeans wondered whether their own cities might be next. To anyone who had been following the issue of Europe's Muslims, the riots were no surprise. The undercurrent of frustration and violence that burst forth had been percolating just below the surface of French society for years. The only surprises involved the episode's interpretations.

Most commentators correctly noted that although many of the young French rioters were Muslims, Islam did not inspire their violence. Some on the political Right in America sought connections between the youths and Al Qaeda, but none were to be found—at least, none involving cooperation with international terror. But on a deeper level, a connection can be drawn between the French rioters and some of Muslim Europe's extremists, such as the July 2005 suicide bombers of London's Underground. Both groups are acting out of a sense of alienation from European society.

Alienation has been fomenting conflicts over symbols. As Germany prepared to host the World Cup in the summer of 2006, Europe's largest, and fully legal, brothel adorned its façade with the flags of all 32 competing nations alongside the image of a prostitute. Outraged that the flags of Saudi Arabia and Iran appeared in this context, Muslim protestors demanded the woman's image be removed. This anger mirrored in the miniature the outburst over perceived anti-Muslim Danish cartoons a few months before.

Acts of extremism always grab the headlines, but headlines tell us little about how the perpetrators came to commit extremist acts. This book steps back from the violence surrounding the Paris riots, the London and Madrid bombings, and the assassination of filmmaker Theo van Gogh in Amsterdam in 2004. Instead, it spotlights the overwhelmingly moderate, religious majority of Europe's Muslim millions. The aim is to reveal the deep ambivalence that many European Muslims feel toward Europe and the United States. In order to do this, I let a wide range of men and women speak for themselves. Many of their names, along with subtle details about their lives, have been changed to protect their identities. To the extent possible, I allowed those I interviewed to review the text of our discussions, to ensure that I had not misrepresented them or their views. Most made almost no substantive changes; a few were more aggressive in fine-tuning the presentation. All of my subjects, regardless of their points of view, proved remarkably forthcoming and eager to tell their tales of life in Muslim Europe.

Although this book focuses on the moderate majority, extremists cannot be disregarded. Their violence undeniably has roots in Europe and the United States and has repercussions on Muslims and non-Muslims in both. One especially chilling act, the grisly, premeditated murder of Van Gogh, is worth a closer look, for although it occurred across an ocean, the attack involved the United States. The murderer targeted a specific victim, yet he made certain to express his hatred of America and what it represented to him. By pure coincidence, the assault took place on the same November day that millions of Americans were going to the polls for an election that would return to office President George W. Bush, whose policies have engendered overwhelming resentment across the Muslim world.

Acknowledgments

I began working on this book immediately after leaving the Policy Planning Staff at the Department of State in 2002. In January 2004, I assembled a book proposal, hired a New York–based literary agent, and began shopping it around. Back then, it proved remarkably difficult to persuade potential publishers that the subject of Europe's Muslims was of growing relevance.

After turning to the Johns Hopkins University Press, we found an editor, Henry Tom, eager to consider the work. Henry asked three scholars to anonymously review the proposal. Each immediately grasped what I wanted to accomplish with this book and recommended publication. Although I do not know the identity of these scholars, I am indebted to them, and to Henry Tom, for their belief in this project. Above all, my agent, Will Lippincott, who invested numerous hours editing the proposal, polishing the prose, and relentlessly pursuing a contract, surely deserves a medal. An author could do no better than to find such a stalwart advocate as Will.

Eugene Mazo first suggested I write this book. Both he and Gwen Parker proved instrumental in the final research phase. I am grateful to them both. So many other colleagues and friends assisted me that I can only give a partial list. They include Gerald Feldman and Beverly Crawford at Berkeley's Institute of European Studies; Harry Kreisler and Stephen Weber, directors of Berkeley's Institute of International Studies; and Margaret Anderson, the outstanding European historian who graciously read and critiqued parts of the manuscript. This work is much the better thanks to their aid and support. Jack Janes and the entire staff of the American Institute for Contemporary German Studies provided me with a base from which I could begin the research, and with their help I obtained generous funding from the Robert Bosch Foundation, the Daimler-Chrysler Foundation, the Smith Richardson Foundation, the Earhart Foundation, and the Kurt A. Körber Foundation. Analysts in the National Intelligence Council and in the Central Intelligence Agency's Strategic Assessment Group generously shared their time and research, as did others within the State Department's Bureau of Intelligence and Research, and the Bureau of European Affairs. The Foreign Policy Research Institute of Philadelphia encouraged me to disseminate some of my ideas both in its journal, *Orbis,* and at a conference they sponsored. Later, Berkeley's Institutes of European and International Studies enabled me to bring the manuscript to completion.

A number of other friends and colleagues provided support along the way. Ben Price not only read many versions of my proposal, he also remained a steadfast believer in this project. As with my previous book, Dominic Hughes turned his logician's mind to the introduction, scrutinizing the presentation and suggesting a crisper structure. Other friends housed me across Europe, assisted with translations, and discussed various ideas with me. These include Nil Demirçubuk, Samuel Gregg, Rebekah Lee, Stephanie Lo, Nadia Marzouki, Elizabeth Miles, Birthe Miller, Ena Pedersen, Rosa Pedersen, Kristin Rebien, and Zhenya Shaposhnikova. My friend and favorite librarian, Michelle Brocius, has helped me through every stage of the research. Michelle possesses a true gift for ferreting out obscure articles, arcane information, fascinating facts, and all the published works I could imagine, plus some I never knew existed. In the final month of writing, I hired a research assistant to help me tie up any loose ends. I was extremely fortunate to find Raakhi Mohan, whose quick mind and positive energy smoothed our ride across the finish line.

As always, my mentors Stanley Hoffmann, Anthony Nicholls, and Stephen Schuker each provided useful feedback and advice. My family has been the greatest support; my mother's thoughtful feedback on drafts, not to mention her loving care and chicken soup, boosted my productivity immensely. My family's encouragement makes everything possible.

Introduction

THE PROLIFIC ASSASSIN

Had it been an ordinary homicide, it would scarcely have been mentioned in the local Amsterdam press, let alone in the global media. But this was no ordinary murder, for the victim was famous, the assailant was Muslim, and the motive appeared to be revenge. Yet despite the intense international coverage, many observers remain unaware that the Dutch-Moroccan murderer had Americans in mind as he planned the gruesome attack.

On the morning of November 2, 2004, while Americans were absorbed in their presidential election, 47-year-old Dutch filmmaker Theo van Gogh, great-grandnephew of the artist Vincent van Gogh, was riding his bicycle to work along an Amsterdam boulevard. Racing up beside him came another bicyclist, a young man dressed in traditional Moroccan garb. Without warning, the stranger suddenly revealed a handgun, aimed, and fired. Swerving off the road, Van Gogh leapt off his bike and ran, but the assailant kept shooting, hitting his target several times. The bullets might have been enough to kill, but the assassin was not finished. He rushed at Van Gogh, wielding a butcher's knife. "Don't do it," Van Gogh pleaded, but without hesitation the stranger stabbed him repeatedly and slit his throat. The incident occurred so quickly that the perpetrator, 26-year-old Mohammed Bouyeri, could still have fled the scene with a chance of escape. Instead, he removed a five-page note from his pocket, placed it over Van Gogh's torso, and plunged a second knife into the bloody corpse, pinning the note to his victim's body. Police chased Bouyeri through a nearby park, exchanged fire, and captured him only after shooting him in the leg. Several days later, the text of Bouyeri's elaborate note was made public. In its conclusion the assassin wrote, "I have no doubt that you, O America"—along with Europe—"will surely fall."

The motive behind Van Gogh's murder seemed clear. Only a few months before, the controversial filmmaker had directed *Submission*, a movie depicting the treatment of women in Islam. The images he showed could hardly have been more inflammatory. The film, which tells the story of a Muslim woman who is beaten by her husband and raped by her uncle, included four nearly naked women, covered only by transparent robes. Their bodies bore whip marks and had Quranic passages affirming a man's right to beat his wife painted across them.

Most commentators assumed that Van Gogh was killed in retaliation for his film. But if Bouyeri was simply taking revenge against Van Gogh for the film, as was widely believed, then why did he address the United States in his murder note? No Americans produced the film. No Americans acted in it, and few Americans even saw it.

Breeding Terrorists

No one is born a terrorist; terrorists are bred. Some are shaped by societal exclusion, convinced they are unwelcome in their own homelands. Others are seduced by sermons of hate, the hapless adherents of perverted preachings. Though all are born neutral, they turn to terror in search of something larger than themselves. Theirs is a spiritual quest gone horribly wrong. Such may have been the case for Van Gogh's assassin. Bouyeri was born and reared in "Satellite City," a working-class Muslim ghetto on Amsterdam's western fringe. A college dropout and one-time journalist, Bouyeri had once written in praise of Holland's multiculturalism, but unable to find steady work, he turned to petty crime. After 9/11, he proved an easy recruit for the Hofstadt Cell, a group of young men who gathered at the El-Tawheed mosque in his neighborhood, reading the radical writings of Syrian cleric Sheikh Abu Khaled. Before long, Bouyeri had donned the traditional Arab robe (the *djallabah*), moved out of his family's apartment, and increasingly saw America and the West as enemies of Islam.

As word of Van Gogh's assassination spread quickly across Amsterdam, some 10,000 Dutch thronged into a city square in shock and protest. In the days that followed, Holland was racked by anti-Muslim attacks. Muslim schools were bombed, children terrorized, and several mosques were set ablaze. To outside observers, the sudden burst of violent animus in a traditionally peaceful country seemed incongruous. But the Van Gogh affair and its aftermath reflect trends underway long before the Madrid train bombings of March 2004 or even America's 9/11. The Dutch case symbolized the social tensions mounting across Europe between a burgeoning young, religious Muslim population, on the one hand, and a fearful, secular, ethnic European populace, on the other.

Seven months after the slaying, Bouyeri was sentenced to life in prison. (There is no death penalty in Holland.) At his trial, he showed no remorse for his crime, insisting he would do it again if given the chance. Clutching a Quran, he declared, "the law compels me to chop off the head of anyone who insults Allah and the prophet."

Europeans were horrified by the brutal murder of Van Gogh and the anti-Muslim violence that followed it. But Bouyeri, unfortunately, is not an aberration. He and his cell are simply the logical result of a long-term cultivation, a process in which many cultural and economic forces are at play. While the West has slept, even after the wake-up call of 9/11, religious extremists from Muslim states have been actively enlisting Western men like Bouyeri, hop-

ing to breed future Osama bin Ladens. Europe's failure to integrate its Muslims, combined with America's battered image in the
Muslim world, has left too many Western Muslims easy prey for
violent dogmas. This volatile European fault line, where Western
failures meet Islamic extremism, is America's Western front in the
war on terror. Until America and Europe adopt new strategies, the
West will increasingly become the incubation ground for breeding
Bin Ladens.

Muslim Europe: The Case for America's Failure

Walk along London's Edgeware Road, where many shops are
Arab-owned, and you will find bookstores with radical literature
calling for jihad against America. Enter some Marseilles homes,
and you can hear preaching against the American way of life. From
the Algerian districts outside of Paris to Turkish enclaves around
Berlin, one can easily tap into a font of hatred toward America.
The Hamburg-based hijackers of 9/11 showed how this hostility
threatens American security. The terrorists who blew up Madrid's
commuter trains on March 11, 2004, were not solely targeting
Spanish civilians; they aimed to gain Spain's withdrawal from Iraq,
in hopes of leaving U.S. forces isolated. The same motives appear
to have inspired the suicide bombers on London's underground
in July 2005. The daily attacks on U.S. soldiers in Iraq—some
traced to European Muslims—are reinforcing the lesson. Europe
is becoming fertile ground for Muslim militancy, and America is
its prime target.

Richard Clarke, the U.S. government's former counterterror-
ism chief, divides the Muslim world into concentric circles. The
largest, outermost circle contains all of the world's 1.3 billion
Muslims, who for the most part are absorbed in their daily lives,
repelled by terror and extremism. The innermost circles consist
of the hardened fanatics, a relatively small group Clarke estimates
at between 50,000 and 100,000. These are the jihadists bent on
the West's destruction, against whom force is the most common

response. But it is the second circle, the middle ring, that is of the greatest concern for a hearts-and-minds campaign. Under the right circumstances, some could be persuaded to lend support to extremism, and others might join terrorist cells. On the other hand, with a wise approach, they could just as readily support America. These Muslims, those in the second circle, are the ones whose support the United States and Europe urgently need to attract.[1]

America's appeal in the Muslim world has rarely been lower. An extensive Pew Research Center survey on global attitudes in 2005 found that majorities in Muslim countries hold negative views of the United States, including in those nations the United States calls its friends. A mere 23 percent of Pakistanis and 21 percent of Jordanians have a favorable opinion of America. A similar Zogby poll in late 2005 found predominantly unfavorable views in Lebanon (66 percent), Jordan (63 percent), the United Arab Emirates (73 percent), Morocco (64 percent), Saudi Arabia (89 percent), and Egypt (85 percent).[2] The Pew organization poll revealed that in Turkey, a NATO member and key U.S. ally, only 17 percent support the U.S.-led war on terror, and in 2004, another Pew survey found that a stunning 31 percent of Turks believed that suicide attacks on Americans in Iraq were justifiable. That same study reported that 55 percent of Jordanians and 65 percent of Pakistanis held favorable views of Bin Laden.[3]

Unfortunately, America's battered image extends throughout Europe, where young Muslims are flocking to extreme views.[4] In one large-scale study of Turkish-German Muslims in their twenties and teens, almost one-third agreed that Islam must become the state religion in every country. Even though they live in Europe, 56 percent declared that they should not adapt too much to Western ways but should instead live according to Islam. Almost 40 percent stated that Zionism, the European Union, and the United States threaten Islam. Perhaps most disturbing, just over one-third insisted that if it serves the Muslim community, then they are ready to use violence against nonbelievers.

America's unpopularity mixed with rising Islamist fundamentalism would be a volatile combination under even the best of circumstances. But added to this mixture is a dangerous demographic ingredient. Muslim populations are exploding. Conservative estimates project that Muslims will be the majority in major German, French, and Dutch cities within a generation. France is already home to 5 million Muslims, almost 10 percent of its total population. Holland, once a safe haven for refugees, will be deporting 26,000 asylum seekers, many of them Muslim, in an effort to stem the rising tide of its Muslim underclass. At the same time, the birthrates of ethnic Europeans are imploding, exacerbating fears that Muslims will one day become a dominant majority. Without coherent, thoughtful integration strategies, the consequences will be dramatic. For Europe, it could mean continent-wide unrest of the kind that racked France in November 2005, when weeks of car burnings raged across French suburbs. It could mean divisive social fragmentation, or a total reordering of the welfare state. For America, the effects could be as perilous as the fraying of transatlantic ties or the recurrence of terrorist attacks at home.

Throughout the EU, more than 15 million Muslims are living, working, raising families, building homes, and starting businesses in lands where capitalism, democracy, and freedom are the norm. American TV shows, films, and products are readily available. American news media is overwhelmingly accessible. If America cannot attract Muslim hearts and minds along this Western front, it has little chance of appealing to them in the Middle East, North Africa, South Asia, or beyond.

Ambi-Americanism

Fortunately, the story of Europe's Muslims and their views of America is far more complex than the raw survey data and violence might suggest. Bouyeri's act in no way represents the sentiments of most of Europe's Muslims. Yet neither are Europe's Muslims enamored of mainstream European or American culture. Theirs is a highly mixed bag of attitudes and beliefs. Torn between two polarizing extremes, Muslim Europe exists in a state of layered ambivalence: ambivalent toward America, toward Europe, and toward mainstream European and American cultural values. Above all, many are uncertain whether and how Islam can coexist within the expanding EU. Will the EU remain a "Christian Club," treating Muslim cultures as alien to the continent, or will Muslims find their future as well-integrated, equal members of European society?

Opinion within Muslim Europe is divided. Although their parents and grandparents retain strong attachments to their ancestral homelands in the Muslim world, Europe's younger Muslims are torn between two new identities. One is European: secular, modern, and middle-class. The other is pan-Islamist: a global community, united under God. Both identities possess powerful appeal, but only one is turning Muslims against America and mainstream European society.

European Muslims are in fact conflicted in their views of America. Because many Muslims are of two minds when it comes to America, it makes little sense to speak of "anti-Americanism." To be truly against America is to hate the entire nation: its people, its products, and its policies. Only a tiny fraction of the world's populace holds such extreme views, and no charm offensives are likely to alter the dogmatic opinion of such fanatics. But the vast majority of Muslims (and indeed many non-Muslims in Europe and around the world, as well) are ambivalent toward America, drawn to some of its characteristics and repelled by others. For this reason, throughout the book I will speak of ambivalent-Americanism, or *ambi-Americanism*, for short.

The roots of *ambi-Americanism* and *ambi-Europeanism* extend far beyond the occupation of Iraq or America's Israel policy. Most Muslims, like most ethnic Europeans, are conflicted toward America. They are attracted by America's appealing traits—its freedoms, openness, technological prowess, educational institutions,

economic opportunities, and some of its cultural exports—but at
the same time they are also repelled by many of its other traits, embodied in its perceived lack of social justice, consumerism, sexual-
ization of women, and putatively hypocritical foreign policies.

There exists among younger European Muslims a growing sense
that Europe and America are spiritually empty. Islam is providing
a powerful magnet to those youth, who crave greater meaning to
their lives. They are finding in Islam a sense of fulfillment that
they have not found in mainstream European culture. Throughout this book, you will meet young Muslims and hear their tales
of discovering the grace of God. Many of these are in fact conversion stories, for while the young people in question were born into
Muslim homes, they were not observant. Once they came of age as
young adults in Europe, they felt the need for something more.

Individual Muslims generally are able to hold their conflicting
opinions of the United States in a precarious balance, but three
proximate factors are tipping the scales against America. First,
fundamentalism is on the march across the continent. Its zeal is
fed by a host of factors, nourished by radical imams in the local mosques and fanatical fatwas propagated on the Web. But the
European states themselves are often fanning the fundamentalist
flames by publishing inflammatory cartoons, enacting anti-terror
legislation which many view as anti-Muslim, or by banning symbols of Islamic faith, such as headscarves in schools and the workplace. Second, high Muslim birth and immigration rates are not
only providing a growing pool from which extremists can draw,
they are also fueling ethnic European fears.

Third, globalization is hindering integration. Networks like the
Qatar-based Al-Jazeera and the Internet bring news of suffering
Muslims to living rooms in Berlin and Paris. As Muslim-produced
news media graphically depict beleaguered Muslims from Chech-
nya to Kashmir, from the Philippines to Afghanistan, and from
Palestine to Iraq, Europe's younger Muslims increasingly iden-

tify with those perceived victims, especially as they themselves feel alienated from European society. They commonly see America as backing their oppressors—the Russians against the Chechens, the Israelis against the Palestinians. Muslim anger and alienation often fuse with a sense of betrayal and the conviction that America is the enemy.

Between Bigots and Bin Ladens

The Van Gogh murder and its violent aftermath revealed the two extremes that threaten to wrench Europe apart. At the one end stand Muslim-hating bigots, bent on excluding or expelling Muslims from European society. At the other are the would-be Bin Ladens, religious zealots who hope to lure young Muslims to their cause. Sandwiched between these bigots and latent Bin Ladens are the overwhelming mass of Europe's 15 million Muslims, searching for their proper place on a continent that does not always feel like home.

This is a book about identities, both of ethnic Europeans and of Europe's Muslims. The first group is struggling to accept that it truly lives in an immigration society, one that is changing and being changed by its new arrivals. As they grapple with all the implications of absorbing "foreign" peoples, Europe undergoes the spasmodic growing pains familiar to Americans from centuries past. The second group is struggling just as much, searching for a Muslim European role on the EU stage. Muslim Europeans are diverse, multi-ethnic, and divided in so many ways. Their future within Europe is anything but certain.

Breeding Bin Ladens profiles some of Europe's younger Muslims at a critical fork in the road: one trail leads them to Western integration, the other sets a course for alienation and possible extremism. It traces their steps as they navigate an identity minefield in search of a cultural "third way."

While this book tells the story of America's image in the Muslim world as seen from inside the second circle, it is also the story of Islam's future in the West. In these pages you will travel to the hotspots where national security and national identity collide—in the streets and mosques of Europe. Through in-depth interviews, I present the honest, anguished, sometimes harsh thoughts and feelings of Europe's younger Muslims, giving Western readers access to a foreign world right in their own backyard.

Chapter 1

LONDON BRIDGES

On the morning of July 7, 2005, Shahara Islam, a lively, outgoing 20-year-old, headed to her job as a cashier at the Cooperative Bank in London's Islington district. Normally, she took the London Underground to work, but partway through her journey the tube stations were closed; the passengers were told there had been an unexpected power surge. Backtracking from the Underground station, she boarded the number 30 bus as an alternate way to get to work. It proved an ill-fated choice.

Among the other passengers who boarded that bus was 18-year-old Hasib Hussain. Born and raised in Britain, Hussain was the son of Pakistani parents. His background was nondescript; he studied business in high school without distinction. He had only attracted notice once in the past, for shoplifting the year before. In 2003, his father had sent him to Pakistan to "gain discipline," and it was there that Hussain became religious. On the morning of July 7, Hussain intended to bomb the northern train in a suicide attack coordinated with similar ones undertaken by three of his friends. But the northern train was out of service that day. He tried to call his friends on his cell phone but was unable to reach them. Needing to improvise his attack, he boarded the number 30 bus. Using a homemade explosive device stuffed into his backpack, Hussain blew himself apart, destroying the bus and killing twelve other passengers with him near Tavistock Square.

Although Shahara was born in Britain, her father, like most of London's Muslims, came from Bangladesh. He worked as a supervisor for London's transport system and had lived in East London for years, raising three children and attending the East London Mosque, where Shahara's grandfather could be seen every Friday in the front row of the main prayer room.

"We never thought something like this could happen here," Dilowar Khan, director of the East London Mosque, later told me. "We thought that suicide bombings were something that happens in the Middle East, in Iraq or Palestine, but not here. We are in shock and disbelief."

It is one week after the attacks, and I have come to London, to the largest mosque in Western Europe, to speak with Khan. When I was planning the trip months earlier, I did not expect the mosque to be swarming with journalists. I pass a Japanese film crew and a pack of British writers on my way up to Khan's office. It was only the night before that mosque officials received confirmation that Shahara was among the 55 victims killed and more than 700 wounded in London's worst attack since the German Luftwaffe air raids more than six decades ago. "There were many tears among the worshippers," Khan said. Shahara was well-liked by everyone who knew her. "Only God fully understands why tragedies occur," he adds. "The Prophet tells us not to delve too deeply into the reasons, because humans cannot understand them."

This statement takes me aback. "But don't we have to at least try to understand these events?" I ask him.

"God gives us the free will to do good or evil," Khan explains. "We cannot see all the connections in human affairs the way that God can. Some things will always be beyond human ability to comprehend."

Certainly one thing I find hard to comprehend is the intense hatred of Muslims which typically surfaces after attacks such as these. Most of the British public has been sympathetic to the Muslim community, Khan says, but a small number of them have sent angry, threatening email to the mosque. Excerpts from those messages follow, but be forewarned. The language is strong and undeniably offensive. It illustrates the fear and hatred which exists toward Muslims in Britain, and these sentiments are echoed by minorities of angry Europeans across the continent. We saw an example of that in normally tolerant Holland following Van Gogh's slaying in 2004.

Some of the messages are short and to the point. One reads simply: "Happy now are you? Look what your religion has encouraged. You are all disgusting." Another note, claiming to be from the far-right British National Party, reads only: "Its now WAR on Muslims throughout Britain." But others are much more explicit. Consider the words of this writer. I have quoted him at length in order to present the full depth and range of his anger.

First of all, what has Islam or Muslims done for England? Nothing. We were fine here thousands of years before your oppressive, women beating people came here and filled our streets. You come here, none of you integrate or make any contributions, and you take our welfare and free medical and send our money back to your shit hole Middle East, where women are still not allowed to vote and are killed if they look at another man. You are not in the fabric of English society, I don't know any English people who would consider Islam a part of English culture, it's you who have come here, you owe us. We owe you nothing. Your damn Quran preaches hate, no wonder we have people bombing—it says seek your enemies relentlessly, and your enemies are anyone who doesn't worship your phony god Allah. I've read your Quran cover to cover many times and it's a hateful document. Muhammad was a pedophile!! Anyone who sleeps with a 9-year-old is a pedophile. It says if you see a Jew or a Christian behind a tree or under a rock, kill him. It says anyone who isn't a Muslim is not your brethren. I'm going to make a personal effort to write to every major English newspaper to expose the horrible teachings of your religion. I've never met a nice Muslim in this country. And I hate how women won't talk to me cause they are so afraid of getting beat by their Muslim men. You cover them in shame. What women would cover themselves head to toe if it wasn't forced by men? We are a free enlightened society, not some barbaric, war mongering, filthy race of people who are still listening to the ramblings of a man from over a thousand years ago! Get with the times! We British want you people out of this country, we hate you. . . . And tell your stinky worshippers to take a fucking shower once in a while, you people are animals.

It may not be entirely unreasonable for the average non-Muslim to believe, mistakenly, that Islam is a violent religion when the perpetrators of these terrorist attacks declare their actions in the name of Islam. (It is, of course, possible to interpret the other Abrahamic religions as condoning violence based on a strict reading of the holy books.) This is one of the most painful dilemmas for the average Muslim, who is being condemned for violent acts which he himself eschews. The writer above faults all Muslims for the acts of a tiny handful. Take a look at the next email for a similar view expressed, one drenched in violence.

I think the killing of 8,000 Muslim men at Srebrenica was a beautiful thing, and it is just the beginning! I long for the day that Christians, Jews and Buddhist wipe your kind off the face of the planet. With great pleasure Buddhist, Jews and Christians will crack your babies skulls against the ground, impale your women on the ends of steel bayonets, use your toddlers and small children as target practice and brutally cut your head off and feed your still warm body to the pigs.

Why do you terrorist bastards not fight like men, but instead hide like sheep behind your women and children. It is just a matter of time before there is open warfare, and the four billion non-Mus-

lims on this planet will send your kind to join your Demon master
Allah in hell!

Until then, may your children feed on bacon fat and your whore
women fuck dogs!

Another email is more succinct, though equally vicious. The
ominous subject line reads: "Look Behind You," and the text is as
follows:

You think you have caught us out . . .

There but the grace of god we will hunt you down and slay you.

Your god is the same higher as ours, you will be finished, I will
make sure that your hatred ends with your families so that the
scourge cannot carry on and your blood will run at our feet until
the liquid is clear, we will drain you,

Your religion does not belong in our country,

I advise you to leave now and we will not rest until our country
is back in our hands, GO HOME and kill your own, of that we do
not care.

Khan comes across as a gentle man, soft-spoken and subdued.
He seems to have read the hate mail with great equanimity. I cannot ask him to explain why ethnic Britons would write such vicious words to a mosque that preaches peace and justice, but I
am curious about what he thinks lies behind the suicide bombers.
The latest news has revealed that all four men were British citizens, three of them born and raised in England. "What do you
think would drive *British* Muslims to commit such horrible acts?" I
asked. "Hopelessness," he answers, without hesitation. "You mean
despair over alienation from British society?"

"No," Khan reflects, "I don't think it has anything to do with
that. I think it has more to do with opposition to the policies of
powerful nations.

"Hmmm. When you say 'the powerful nations,' I'm assuming
you mean the United States, and perhaps Britain. Is that right?"

Khan's voice is calm and steady as he lays out his views for me. "Muslims are not supposed to be nationalists. The belief in one God binds us to the umma (the global community of Muslims). When British Muslims see the suffering of other Muslims around the world, they experience that suffering as if it were their own. These suicide bombings come from the despair over our helplessness to stop the suffering of Muslim brothers and sisters around the world. These bombers feel that they must do something with their lives to help."

"Then you think it's really about Iraq, as they're saying in the papers?"

"The British people are tolerant, sensible, and responsible. Until Iraq, the British government was also looked up to and admired in some ways. Many Muslims prefer to come here to live, not to the United States. Now, the situation may be changing." Khan's suspicions are partly corroborated by a large-scale opinion poll on global attitudes. When asked where they would advise a young person to move in order to live a good life, the majority of respondents chose Australia, Canada, Great Britain, and Germany ahead of the United States. The survey examined attitudes worldwide, but a number of predominantly Muslim countries were included in the sample.[1]

Khan may have also been right about the bombers' motivations. Seven weeks after my interview with him, Al-Jazeera broadcast a macabre video in which Mohammed Siddique Khan, the suspected ringleader of the attacks, explained his actions to the British public. Having blown himself up two months earlier, his message had an even more ghoulish effect. "I and thousands like me are forsaking everything for what we believe. Our driving motivation doesn't come from tangible commodities that this world has to offer. This is how our ethical stances are dictated. Your democratically elected governments perpetuate atrocities against my people, and your support of them makes you directly responsible, just as I am directly responsible for protecting and avenging my Muslim brothers and sisters. Until we feel security, you will be our target."[2]

"So what is the attitude toward the United States among most of your congregants?" I asked Director Khan.

"The U.S. government wants to dominate the world's resources, including those of the Middle East," Khan explains. "It wants to insure that Muslim nations never become powerful. Most Muslims believe that Israel controls U.S. foreign policy."

"Why do they think that?"

"For one reason, it's hard for us to understand why America gives more foreign aid to Israel than to all of Africa. We are not against Jewish people at all. It is political Zionism that we dislike. The logic of Zionism seems to be that the land can only belong to the people who can prove they were there first. But if you follow this logic, then America must be returned to the native tribes."

"What do you really mean when you say that Israel controls U.S. foreign policy?"

"I mean that there is a powerful pro-Israel lobby in America that is skilled at influencing policy. There are wealthy businessmen and powerful politicians who support pro-Israel policies. Alternative views have little chance of gaining ground. There is a strong feeling of ill-will toward the United States among many Muslims because of its unjust policies."

These are the views of one of Britain's most prominent, moderate Muslim leaders. They were not spoken with hatred or anger, but in a matter-of-fact tone. They do not suggest an adamant opposition to all things American; they represent instead ambi-Americanism. Khan is a man with deep qualms about American policies and the values that he perceives those policies to reflect.

Khan's perspective on the bombers' motivations is reflected in the words of some Muslim youths in Leeds, the town north of London where three of the four July 7 attackers lived and planned their assault. Friends of Shehzad Tanweer, one of the suicide bombers, told the *New York Times* that while they did not support what their friend did, they understood what drove him to it. "He was sick of it all, all the injustice and the way the world is going," said one young man. Another added, "Why, for example, don't they ever take a moment of silence for all the Iraqi kids who die?"

In Birmingham, England's second-largest city, which has a major Muslim population, the *Times* interviewed Dr. Waheed, a practicing psychiatrist, who, along with growing numbers of well-educated British Muslims, has embraced a more radical Islamic movement. Hizb ut-Tahrir, or Party of Liberation, seeks to restore the caliphate and return to a strict, traditional Islamic lifestyle. Waheed remarked, "We know that the killing of innocents is forbidden, but we don't see two classes of blood; the blood of Iraqis is just as important to us as English blood."[3]

Hizb ut-Tahrir is the creation of Syrian-born cleric Sheik Omar Bakri. He established it in Britain after being expelled from Saudi Arabia for his extremist views. Britain's tolerant laws enabled Bakri and men like him to promulgate their creed to young British Muslims. It is unclear how many people have been influenced by his brand of extremism. Following the London bombings, Bakri was quoted as saying, "He [Bin Laden] is showing that he can use British Muslims, who are living on your own doorstep, to harm you. He doesn't have to bring people all the way from Medina and Saudi Arabia to fly over here. . . . If this attack was Al Qaeda, then I think it can be considered a great success for them."[4]

While Hizb ut-Tahrir is striving to create true Islamic states, the East London mosque hopes to build bridges with British society. The mosque itself is a massive complex, four stories high and occupying thousands of square meters. After my meeting with Director Khan, Shamsul, a young British man of Bangladeshi ancestry, offers me a private tour of the facilities. A large empty room on one of the upper floors will soon become a major research library holding works on Islamic thought and teaching. Another section is designated for an Islamic radio station aimed at the greater London area. One whole floor is filled with classrooms offering Arabic and English instruction, computer skills, and Quranic education to the general community. Other classrooms are filled with young children. The mosque has received accreditation from the British government to serve as an official school. Like Catholic schools in the United States, the mosque offers national curricula courses in math, science, and the humanities, while also providing additional religious instruction.

"Shamsul," I ask, "do you think that separating Muslim children out from the mainstream of British schools makes it harder for them to integrate into society?"

He shakes his head definitively. "No," he says, "they still learn to integrate because Islam encourages community involvement. They learn that they are connected to all people, not just Muslims."

The main prayer room is impressive, to say the least. While regular Friday services may draw four to five thousand worshippers, a holiday service can find between six and seven thousand Muslims gathering here to pray. For these events a separate annex is used. There are also reception rooms for weddings and special events. Space has even been established for a restaurant that will serve halal products. When Shamsul mentions the restaurant, I remember my thirst. It is a hot and sticky afternoon. For some years I have been wanting to try Qibla Cola, the Muslim-made competitor to Coca-Cola®. I need only ask and Shamsul provides me with a can.

Qibla Cola is designed to look like Coke with its red and white motif. I'll write more about it and my interview with the company's spokesman in the chapter on economic jihad, but for now my attention is drawn to the ingredients.

ETHICAL CONTENT
Added Injustice: 0%
Exploitation: 0%
Artificial Morals: 0%
Inflated Claims: 0%
Conscience Free

To me, Qibla Cola tastes less sweet than Coke, and definitely different from its larger rivals. "Do you prefer this to Coke?" I ask Shamsul.

"Actually, I don't drink either," he grins. "I don't really like fizzy drinks."

Across the street a new bank has opened, the Islamic Bank of Britain. Director Khan told me that the mosque was considering switching its account to IBB, so I walk past its shiny façade. The bank is housed in a glass and steel building highlighted by modest neon signs. Above the entrance a sign declares that this is the United Kingdom's first bank to comply with sharia (Islamic law), and the slogan states simply, "It's Your Choice."

The East London mosque has a mission. It wants to build bridges between faiths in Britain. With the most expansive mosque and Islamic center in Western Europe at its disposal, plus its own radio station planned to follow,[5] those bridges ought to be erected with relative ease. But a host of factors are working against its efforts. A few ethnic Britons want Muslims out of the country. On the other extreme, a group of Muslims wants to build an Islamic state in Europe. Yet both these obstacles may prove meager when compared to the more vexing problem that growing numbers of young British Muslims feel alienated from and ambivalent about British society. A *Guardian* poll found that while most British Muslims denounce violence, only one-third said that they wanted more integration into mainstream society. This trend among the young is mirrored across the continent. As non-mainstream alternatives continue to arise—Muslim colas, Islamic banks, separate schools, or closed communities—how will Dilowar Khan and the average, moderate Muslim build bridges into mainstream European society? And if even Muslims like Khan hold such views about America, believing it to be a country that wants to dominate the resources of Muslim states, what kind of bridges will the United States have to Muslim Europe?

Faisal is a British-Muslim of Arab descent. Now in his early thirties, he sports a stylish beard and dapper dress. Well-educated and thoughtful, he follows Arab affairs closely. He is also devout in his religious observance, praying five times daily, keeping the Ramadan fast, and doing charitable works. For several years Faisal worked in London for the embassy of a Muslim country.[6] He tells me that the corruption of Islamic values he witnessed was at times profound. Some men sent to Britain as official emissaries spent embassy funds on prostitutes. Others simply wasted vast sums on extravagant meals and unnecessary luxuries. "Some of the same Muslims who pretend to be the most pious are the ones who defy Mohammed's teachings in their own lives," Faisal says.

"I'll never forget September 11," Faisal continues. "Everyone in the Embassy was absolutely gleeful. People were almost cheering when the second plane struck the other tower. They acted as if America deserved this tragedy, like it finally got a poke in the eye for its arrogance. And then, a weird thing happened over the next few days. When it became clear that Muslims were responsible, they all started to deny that Muslims could have been behind it. They went around insisting it was an Israeli conspiracy. Yet a few days before they seemed almost proud of what was done."

"I've had a lot of people tell me they thought it was a Jewish or a CIA conspiracy. What did you think about 9/11?"

"It was a horrible, disgraceful attack of barbarism, and Muslims were responsible. We should face that fact and denounce it."

I pursued this, saying: "It seems that no matter where I go around Europe, whether it's London or Hamburg, Ljubljana or Prague, whether they are Sunni or Shia, young or old, educated or not, the Muslims I meet all oppose the United States' actions in Iraq. In your work and in your personal life, you have had more exposure to Americans than many of those I've met. You read widely in English and know the many American points of view. What's your view?"

"Saddam was a terrible butcher. He deserved to be killed. But the U.S. should have found another way to do it than invasion. The American government doesn't seem to understand how much Muslims hate what they have done. The whole thing with weapons of mass destruction looked unbelievable even before the invasion. They've just killed a lot of innocent people and it wasn't necessary. It looks to many Muslim eyes as very unjust."

Before the London underground attacks of 2005, Europe was shocked by the Madrid train bombings in 2004. Almost immediately after the Madrid tragedy, British authorities arrested eight young Muslim men suspected of plotting terrorist attacks. Contrary to the usual profile of angry new immigrants, all of the suspects were British-born and lived in suburban, middle-class areas, some of them raising families. Their profiles were not unlike those of some of the July 7 suicide bombers. In order to preempt an expected spike in Islamophobia, the Muslim Council of Britain launched a vigorous public relations offensive. Based in London, the MCB claims to be the UK's representative Muslim umbrella body, with over 400 affiliated national, regional, and local organizations, mosques, charities, and schools. In an email sent to every imam and chair of every mosque in Britain, the MCB's secretary-general called upon Muslim leaders to preach the peaceful ways of Islam, cooperate with authorities in any reasonable way, and "to develop active contacts with other faith communities and civic organizations in order to help maintain social peace and good community relations."

Since 9/11, the MCB, like Muslims across Europe, has been at pains to distance itself from Islamic extremists. It is fighting an uphill battle, given the media's proclivity for sensational headlines and generalizations. Each time a British broadsheet reports on attacks with headlines such as "Islamic Bomb Plot Foiled," British Muslims and community relations are set back. Part of the MCB's energies have been targeted toward correcting public misconceptions about Islam. As the MCB's secretary-general put it in a widely circulated open email letter:

Following the criminal terrorist attack on the Madrid trains, and despite our immediate, public and unequivocal condemnation of those atrocities, some, however, continue to associate Islam with terrorism by using such misleading terms as "Islamic terrorist." The words of the Quran are clear: "He who killed any person, unless it be a person guilty of manslaughter, or of spreading chaos in the land, should be looked upon as though he had slain all mankind, and he who saved one life should be regarded as though he had saved the lives of all mankind."(5:32)[7]

But the backlash was unavoidable. Within days of the Madrid attacks, more than forty graves in a Muslim cemetery in southeast London were desecrated. In Guilford, a young Muslim girl was abducted by a man who slashed crosses into her hands and arms with a razor blade.[8]

After the 2005 London bombings, however, the calculus changed. When Prime Minister Tony Blair announced sweeping new anti-terror laws, mainstream Muslim organizations like the MCB feared that their right to free speech was under assault. Blair called for the banning of groups like Hizb ut-Tahrir, but the MCB objected. Declaring itself no fan of Hizb ut-Tahrir's brand of political Islam, the MCB nonetheless viewed the proposed ban as an encroachment on basic civil liberties. The subtext to its objections was feared that their right to speak out against British and American policies in Iraq would be curtailed. On August 5, 2005, the MCB announced that it was "seeking clarification from the government to ensure that expressions of support for people who are living under brutal military occupation is not to be outlawed. That would be completely unacceptable. Our faith of Islam commands us to speak out against injustice wherever it occurs."[9]

The MCB has a vested stake in defending its right to criticize the perceived oppression of Muslims at home or abroad, especially in Palestine or Iraq. It is both a matter of civil liberty within a democracy and a question of religious duty to protest perceived injustice. The MCB has repeatedly condemned America's Middle East policies. In March 2004, when Sheikh Ahmad Ismail Yasin, the spiritual leader of Hamas, was killed in an Israeli helicopter attack, the MCB immediately declared, "We hold the international community and the United States directly responsible for allowing the Israeli Occupation Forces to continue with its policy of wanton killing and terrorizing of Palestinian civilians. No amount of military force and assassinations will bring about a Final Solution to the 'Palestinian problem.'"[10]

One month later, when U.S. forces bombed the Abdul Aziz al-Samarrai mosque in Fallujah, Iraq, the MCB decried America by claiming that the United States Army had embarked on "a murderous Israeli-style siege of Fallujah." They continued, "Yesterday's bombing of the Mosque complex combined with the horrific killings of over 290 Iraqi civilians, including small children, in Fallujah in the past few days have shocked Muslims worldwide."[11]

So here's the rub. Moderate, mainstream Muslim groups demand their right to free speech, in part to criticize (and potentially to change) Britain's and America's foreign policies. But the demand for free speech butts up against the general public's fears of radical, political Islam. Moderate Muslims insist, as anyone should in a democracy, on their right to speak out against policies they find unjust, but radical groups like Hizb ut-Tahrir could be protected under the same free-speech tenets. The circle, in theory, could be easily squared. Those who call for violence should not deserve the right to free speech; those who call for justice without violence should be free to speak their minds. How Britain, and indeed the rest of Europe, will resolve this and similar debates remains to be played out. But if moderate Muslims, those in the second circle, are to have their say, they will do it in the democratic way, at the polls. And as their numbers continue to rise, they are certain to alter Europe's political landscape.

To Overthrow a King

If Tony Blair's New Labour could have created an ideal candidate, Oona King would have been it. A smart, young, mixed-race woman, dubbed by the media as one of "Blair's Babes," she seemed sure to hold onto her safe seat in Bethnal Green, a multicultural district of East London in 2005. King had won the seat in 2001, capturing a remarkable 51 percent of the vote in a six-way race. But Bethnal Green is also 40 percent Muslim. It is Dilowar Khan and the East London mosque's district. At first glance, this might have seemed a source of strength, but King's position on a single issue turned the Muslim population against her.

King was born in Sheffield in 1967. Her mother was Jewish, of Hungarian and Scotch-Irish descent; her father, Preston King, was African-American. His brother served as counsel for Martin Luther King Jr., and their father was a founder of the National Association for the Advancement of Colored People. When Preston won a scholarship to study at the London School of Economics, he was eager to attend. In order to leave the United States, however, he needed to complete official forms legally exempting him from the U.S. military's draft program. King agreed, but only if the American officials would address him with the title "Mr.," as they did with white students. The officials refused, addressing him instead as "Preston." In protest, King never signed the forms, but he did earn his degree at the LSE. Upon returning to America, he was arrested for draft evasion. When the judge imposed an impossibly high bail, the black community in Atlanta raised the money. Preston King then fled to England, where he remained for decades. Nearly a lifetime later, the 94-year-old judge who had convicted King years before wrote to President Clinton admitting that King's conviction had been based solely on racism. In 2000, President Clinton granted Preston King an official pardon.

Oona King inherited much of her father's zeal for justice. With her record of promoting women's rights and labor issues, Oona

King had undeniably impressive credentials to stand as a defender of justice and equality. What she lacked in 2005, from the voters' point of view, was the right stand on Iraq.

Third-party candidates typically confront stiff odds, but a candidate from a newly formed third party is usually the longest of long shots. That did not deter George Galloway, a fiery, audacious speaker who was expelled from the Labour Party because of his vocal opposition to the Iraq invasion. Rather than retiring into obscurity, this spirited maverick formed the Respect Party and chose to challenge Labour in the heart of one of its strongholds. Galloway galvanized support around the very issue on which Oona King was vulnerable. Seizing on King's support for Blair's Iraq policy, Galloway flew to the predominantly Muslim nation of Bangladesh and attacked the Blair government for deceiving the British people and launching an illegal war. Precisely as expected, Galloway's remarks reverberated back home, hitting the local East London Bangladeshi newspapers. King, who once held a commanding lead, now looked to be in trouble.

King still held the advantage of incumbency. Despite the political pressures to change her view, King never wavered in her support for the war. In 1991, she had been part of a parliamentary inquiry into Saddam's regular torturing of Iraqi civilians and vowed then that the dictator had to be deposed by any means. So part of her campaign strategy in 2005 was to remind voters that Saddam's cruelty was against Muslims, who were better off with Saddam gone—the same argument that President Bush has repeatedly made. It had no sway over East London's Muslims, Britain's Muslims, Europe's Muslims, or, from what most surveys can ascertain, Muslims in the umma. No other single act in recent years has done more to turn Muslims against the United States than the invasion and occupation of Iraq. George Galloway understood this clearly and set about exploiting King's Achilles' heel. In the weeks before the vote, King's once commanding lead began to shrink.

But then, an unexpected twist occurred. Scarcely two weeks

prior to election day, Galloway, accompanied by his daughter, was speaking at a tenant's association meeting when a group of some forty Muslim men burst into the room. Calling him a false prophet and locking the door behind them, the men demanded that Galloway withdraw from the race, apparently believing that a non-Muslim such as Galloway should not be drawing Muslim supporters. It appeared that these men opposed the democratic process and sought to prevent Muslims from voting. Two police constables soon arrived on the scene and escorted the candidate out of the building.

Curiously, Galloway was not their only target. Earlier that same day, a similar mob disrupted a meeting of the Muslim Council of Britain by shouting insults at Sir Iqbal Sacranie, the MCB's secretary-general. The protesters distributed leaflets urging Muslims not to vote in the election. The fliers read in part: "Voting for any political party . . . will guarantee your seat in hellfire forever." Police believe that the group that harassed Sacranie was linked to the group that harassed Galloway. Believing he still retained the support of a majority of Bethnal Green's moderate Muslims, Galloway did not withdraw.

On election night, May 5, 2005, after a hair-raisingly close election, the final votes were tallied. In this four-way race, votes split between the three established parties—Labour, Conservative, Liberal Democrat—and the new Respect Party. The winner would not require 50 percent plus one, but merely a plurality of votes, meaning a higher percentage than any of the other parties. The once dominant Labour Party netted 34 percent of the vote, while the Respect Party squeaked ahead with 36 percent, enough to be declared the winner. George Galloway triumphantly proclaimed, "Oona King boasted that she was going to finish me off. The defeat was not her defeat this evening. It was a defeat for Tony Blair, New Labour and all their betrayals." Galloway hung his victory squarely on the issue that fueled his campaign. Mincing no words, he announced, "Mr. Blair, this is for Iraq. The defeat you've suffered—and all the other defeats New Labour has suffered this evening—is for Iraq. All the people you killed, all the lies you told, have come back to haunt you. The best thing the Labour Party can do is sack you tomorrow morning." Apparently, there were many Londoners, both Muslim and non-Muslim, who agreed.

Given its newness, its relative lack of funds compared to the established parties, and its seemingly single-issue nature, it was a good night for Respect. The party came in second in the London districts of East Ham and West Ham, with 21 and 20 percent of the vote, respectively, and third in Poplar and Canning Town, with 17 percent. In Birmingham, home to the next highest Muslim population after London, the Respect Party candidate Salma Yaqoob ended the night in second with 27 percent of the vote in the Sparkbrook and Heath areas. Galloway insisted, "You ain't seen nothin' yet!"

Regardless of whether the Respect Party remains a force in British politics, King's defeat, mainly by British Muslims, reveals a key window into Europe's future. It shows that Europe's Muslims, if given the opportunity, will actively participate in the democratic process in order to make their voices heard. It reveals the potential for politicians to capitalize on that growing constituency. And above all, it exposes the deep passion that Muslims feel toward the umma: their brothers and sisters in Islam, no matter how far-flung that religious family may be. Iraq heightened the animosity of Muslims against the British and American supporters of the Iraq war. Even if American troops are withdrawn from Iraq, the effects of invasion and occupation, the suffering inflicted upon so many thousands of average Iraqis, will not easily be forgotten. This is especially true for the growing numbers of young, religious Muslims in Europe who intend to make their mark there.

Islam is undergoing a revival across Europe. As young European Muslims seek their place within the EU, many are finding in

Islam a different kind of purpose and identity than their parents' generation did. They are becoming more devout and more intense in their religion than their parents had been. These newly awakened younger Muslims are still in the minority among their Muslim European peers, but signs indicate that they may not remain the minority for very long.

Chapter 2

ISLAMIC AWAKENINGS

When Ayaan Hirsi Ali arrived in Holland, her prospects looked anything but bright. A native of Mogadishu, Somalia, she and her family were forced to flee the country after her father, a politician in the opposition, was threatened. But for young Ayaan, her new surroundings were hardly improved. Her family fled to Saudi Arabia, where she was forced to veil and spend most of her life indoors. After her father pledged her in marriage to a cousin she did not even know, Hirsi Ali decided to escape again, this time entirely on her own.

At age 22, she landed in Amsterdam, took a job as a cleaning woman, and began to build a new life. Few would have suspected that within ten years she would master the Dutch language, earn a university education, gain a reputation for her writings on female exploitation, and rise to become one of the country's best-known political figures. Fewer still could have predicted that her fame would come at so high a price. Hirsi Ali is once more forced to live indoors—this time in fear of her life.

Hirsi Ali's prominence, as well as her controversy, traces back to the time she spent working as a translator for the Dutch immigration service. There she quickly discovered the extent of violence against Muslim women occurring in Holland and began to write about the many exploited women she encountered. These were Muslim immigrants who did not speak Dutch, were often raped and beaten by their husbands or relatives, and who had little chance of escape. In exposing this social problem, Hirsi Ali drew the ire of some Muslim men, who felt she was slandering the reputation of Muslim men and desecrating Islam. Their anger, though certainly not their violence, is understandable, since she did use highly inflammatory language about the Prophet, calling him a pedophile and declaring herself an ex-Muslim. That was when the death threats began.

Mohammed Bouyeri's bloody note—the one he pinned to Van Gogh's corpse—not only declared that America and Europe would fall, it also railed against Hirsi Ali for writing and co-producing *Submission*. Bouyeri proclaimed to Hirsi Ali, "You have turned your back on truth and are marching with the soldiers of evil." He continued, "Islam will be victorious through the blood of the martyrs. . . . There will be no mercy shown to the purveyors of injustice. Only the sword will be lifted against them."

Bouyeri and Hirsi Ali represent two extremes for Muslim Europe. One is a violent fanatic; the other a wholly secular, mainstream feminist. Bouyeri was 26 at the time of his crime; Hirsi Ali was 33. But for most young Muslims across Europe, Islam is not compatible with either extreme. Rather, it is a religion of balance that emphasizes justice in all realms of life. And for growing numbers of young people, Islam is becoming a more significant force in their lives.

Most non-Muslim Europeans and Americans have difficulty comprehending Islam's tremendous appeal, mainly because so little of what it means to be a Muslim is known to non-believers. The extremists like Bouyeri and the London suicide bombers have deepened the chasm of misunderstanding that already prevailed before violent extremists began targeting European capitals. But a close-up look at one of the most pivotal religious experiences a

Muslim can have, an experience that often proves life changing, helps illuminate the religion's transformative force. It is even more comprehensible when seen through the eyes of a young, British Muslim woman.

On the Hajj

Mahsa is not your average British woman. For that matter, she is not average in many respects. Born in Iran, she moved with her parents to England at age 14. After high school she earned her bachelor's, master's and doctoral degrees at Oxford, with an engineering focus in optics. Now 26, Mahsa does not wear the hijab; she dresses in Western garb, though nothing flashy. She is a gentle, plainspoken woman with a scientist's mind and a pleasant but serious demeanor. She is, by any account, a well-integrated European Muslim with an impressive education. The fact that Mahsa was drawn to Islam in her early adulthood says much about the religion's powerful appeal.

Muslims are commanded to perform five essential tasks in life: professing Allah as the one, true God; giving to charity; praying five times daily; fasting during the month of Ramadan; and at least once in their lifetime making the pilgrimage to Mecca. Each year, roughly 20,000 British Muslims make the hajj, and many more travel to Mecca from across Europe.[1] As the number of European Muslims who earn hard currency in euros continues to rise, more will have the economic means to make the trip. In 2004, Mahsa made her pilgrimage for the first time, and her description offers a window into what is for non-Muslims a poorly understood practice. I asked her to share her own hajj experience, and she eagerly agreed.

> *Mahsa:* My dad and I started off in Medina and were there for a week. The Prophet's mosque is beautiful, huge and where I have felt most humble. I had never felt that small in my life and it was a strange feeling. I guess most of it was due to the fact that the

Prophet, many members of his family, and his companions had spent years there and some were buried there right in the mosque or next to it. Every time that I entered the mosque (five times a day for the prayers), I had this overwhelming feeling of being very privileged to be there and of being so small in the grand scheme of things.

ZS: The hajj is a time for prayer and reflection, right? So what are the prayer times like?

Mahsa: The prayer times were simply one of the most beautiful scenes in both Mecca and Medina, especially in Mecca. You suddenly see a wave of people going in the same direction as if there is a big magnet in the middle and people are little iron files. You never have to ask for directions to the mosques . . . you just follow people.

ZS: I know that thousands of Muslims converge on Mecca from around the world. Can you tell me what that's like?

Mahsa: The pilgrims, themselves, are one of the most interesting dimensions of the pilgrimage. I was thinking that this must be the only event where people from virtually every single country, from the poorest villages in Africa to the most affluent parts of Europe, come together for a single purpose. Our religious leader in the group said something that was very interesting. There is nothing about Mecca that would make it a tourist attraction. It is baking hot for most of the year (around 25°C when we were there, the best time to go). It is surrounded by rocky mountains and has the single miracle of Zamzam water[2] for drinking water. . . . The rest comes from surrounding areas. So people come for the sole reason that God has called them, and you really do see that. Rule number one was that in order to pray inside the mosques and not in the courtyards, you had to be there at least 45 minutes before the call to prayer. It was a real art finding a place to squeeze into when we were late. I loved sitting next to random people and talking to them.

I was often mistaken for an Arab as I dressed like one and had lots of non-conversations with Indonesians and Pakistanis and sometimes Africans. The really interesting thing was that everybody insisted on speaking their own language, and it was usually sign language that was the most effective.

Iranians were so funny, as I am sure were the others, and I only understood Persian and English. I liked Indonesians best because they always took pity on me when I looked for a place to stand in and they always shook hands after every prayer. The scene after the prayers was fascinating. It almost made me cry every time. People with hands in the air were supplicating to God in zillions of different languages and once again, there was just the One that was being called. The most important point that I deduced from hajj is that it is a practice in monotheistic worship. . . . All the traditions and rituals are Abrahamic, the founder of monotheistic faiths.

ZS: I can imagine it's a bonding experience to be with so many different people all there for a single purpose, and all going through the same acts of worship. Tell me about the rituals you perform.

Mahsa: Before entering Mecca, you have to prepare in a special way. It is sacred grounds and you can't just turn up. So you change into white clothing. Men wrap two towels around them because their clothes cannot be tailored, and women can wear anything but most wear white. We went to the Shajareh mosque in Medina to say the special supplication before embarking on our journey to Mecca. This is what the Prophet had done on his hajj and so most pilgrims follow the tradition. I was completely overwhelmed by the saying of the supplication which is essentially that Oh, Allah, You have invited me and I have answered Your call.

I just could not stop crying while saying these words as I felt completely unworthy of such a responsibility. During the time that you leave in this state until you arrive in Mecca and perform *umrah,* the "small hajj," you are not allowed to do 23 things, of which I remember not killing anything including plants and flies, not looking

in the mirror, not using fragrances, not wearing makeup nor pluck-
ing hair, no swearing, no fighting, not even a dirty look—basically
anything that would disturb peace and anything that reminds you
of who you are in terms of your looks, status, etc. The amazing
thing is that you actually don't really care about these things on this
trip, and you really leave "you" behind.

We arrived in Mecca at around 2 am and went straight to "the
mosque" (where Kaaba is) to perform the small hajj. I was actually
quite nervous about seeing Kaaba, as I had heard how people go
completely numb at the sight of God's house. I was in fact fine, and
all I could do was fall down and prostrate in front of the house. It
looks much more distant on TV than it really is. It is located in a
"dip" and the area around it is much smaller than I had imagined.

I thought two things then: one, that this is a lesson—God is
much nearer than we imagine, and two, that it is so simple. The
structure is a directionless box, it is simply a sign that attracts 3
million pilgrims every year and towards which millions more pray
everyday. I loved watching people circumambulate the house while
others were praying in every direction (wherever you turn you see
God). Dad and I and a group of others started the circumambulation and went around seven times, as did Hagar and all the proph-
ets. You get so absorbed in the crowd that is walking with you that
you don't actually make much effort to walk. You are simply a drop
in the sea and you are lost in the Oneness again. The whole time
people were praying aloud and saying prayers for each turn to make
sure that they don't lose count, but I didn't feel like doing anything
but praising God and thinking this really is what I imagine to be
immersion in One.

ZS: What about the other stages? There are separate parts to the
whole hajj, right?

Mahsa: There is another stage, called "the effort," of the small hajj.
This was walking between two mountains seven times as Hagar had
done in search of water for Ismail. I think this walk symbolizes a

person's effort in life. That you have to be active and to work in this life but have faith in the reward. Hagar didn't find water between the mountains but she did find Zamzam next to Ismail when she returned to him. After the walk you are done with the small hajj and you can once again do the things that were forbidden to you.

We spent the next few days going to prayers and generally spent a lot of time in the mosque. The "big hajj" started on the Friday and we got back into the white clothes. The big hajj essentially consists of three stages and lasts for about four to five days. These days were probably the simplest and yet the most meaningful days of my life. You spend time living in tents and there is nothing in particular that you need to do except for the last two days, and even then, they take one hour maximum. The first day is the day of "knowing." I interpret this as the day of getting to know yourself and it is meant to be a day of reflection on all that you have done in life. The most amazing feature is the identical tents (some don't even have tents) and the identical people. You really can't tell the rich from the poor or the educated from the illiterate. Everybody looks the same, clad in white, and everybody has equal facilities . . . all equal in God's eyes. I spent the day under the sky and roamed around the tents and could just imagine that this is how Judgment Day would be. After sunset, we set off for the next stop, and spent the night there. Women left after midnight but men stayed behind. Practically all the men caught a cold as the nights were freezing and all they had was a couple of towels around them. This is again, a thinking stage and where you collect little stones.

We reached the third stage (Menna) at around 2 am. Our luggage had been taken there before us. As soon as we got to Menna, we were taken to stone the "big Satan." There is a place where there are three pillars, small, medium, and large. On the first night, you stone the big pillar and the following two days, you stone all three. Seven times each, and that is why we collected stones before. The pillars symbolize Satan when he appeared three times to Abraham when he was ordered to slaughter Ismail. He stoned the Satan all three times and that is what we do, but in fact, in every stone, re-count our own faults and weaknesses and stone those. We repeat to reaffirm. On the second day, I got hit in the lip and my dad's glasses were broken, but nothing serious. Unfortunately, on that day a lot of people were killed in a stampede which was apparently due to a fight that had broken out between street peddlers. After the stoning on the second day, a sheep was slaughtered for every pilgrim and we celebrated Eid [the festival that follows the end of Ramadan]. I think you keep repeating the slaughter every year to remind you of the sacrifices and promises that you have to make in Islam.

We got back to Mecca in normal clothes and flew back to Dubai a couple of days later.

ZS: Looking back on it from the perspective of several months' time, how important would you say the hajj was?

Mahsa: I guess I really recommend that people take time to make the hajj when they are young. It really is a life-changing experience, and it had best happen when there is still time to change.

Growing Up Muslim and European

I wanted to know what Mahsa's experiences were like growing up in Britain. Though she came to England at age 14, she adapted quickly enough, excelled in school, and made friends. Were her teenage years and early twenties troubled or smooth sailing? How did she accommodate the sometimes taxing demands of being from a distinctly religious background in a Christian or secular society? Her comments, and those of the other young Muslims profiled below, shed light on the difficulties young Muslims can face integrating.

My parents did have a big influence as they are both practicing, but I only really found faith around age 21. So although I subscribe to the Shia school of thought, I strongly disagree with the common practice of it in Iran and elsewhere, and am in that respect nondenominational. [The majority of the world's Muslims belong to the Sunni sect. The Shiites, 10–15 percent of Muslims, are a majority only in Iran, Iraq, Bahrain, and Azerbaijan.]

I guess the question of being a Muslim in Europe and its implications is a difficult one. A lot of the times I identified myself as an Iranian despite being a British citizen . . . so I didn't and don't face the problem that many of my peers are facing, namely, belonging to neither the British nor their parents' culture. I don't particularly feel like I fit into the "Iranian box" either, but that is the culture that I identify with most. . . . I think that those brought up in two or several places are a bit like mixed-race people . . .

The problems I faced in Europe as a practicing Muslim were not your "average" problems of discrimination, etc., as many would mistake me for a southern European and I sort of "blended in." They were pretty much the kind of problems that anyone not following the mainstream culture experienced. For example, I didn't like the heavy drinking culture prevalent in undergraduate Oxford life, drunken men's behavior towards women, and the fact that college social life revolved so much around the college bar.

I found that people respected the fact that I disappeared for prayers, but not many were willing to discuss it. Maybe religion is not a trendy subject to talk about, especially among scientists, but maybe they didn't like religiosity and were simply too polite to say so.

I resent the fact that people automatically assume that you are not a practicing Muslim if you don't look like one.

Islamic societies of Berkeley and Oxford [Mahsa spent one year studying engineering at the University of California at Berkeley] were too conservative for my liking and I hear it is pretty much the same elsewhere . . . but, it was a good medium for meeting like-minded fellow Muslims, and to at least celebrate religious festivals. Although most of my close friends in Europe, and in fact in Iran, are non-Muslims, I really appreciate having Muslim friends around with whom I feel at ease to talk about faith and to be inspired by their faith.

Velija is 29, and at 6′7″ is a giant even by German standards. He was born in Bremerhaven in northern Germany, the son of a guest worker from Bosnia. Trained as a banker but unable to find work, Velija, who is blind, supports his wife and two young daughters as a drummer in a local band.

"My father was not a religious man. He drank alcohol, ate pork, and lived his life like a secular worker, both in Bosnia and in Germany. But when I went blind at age eight, my father became convinced that this was punishment for his sins. An imam told him that God does not strike you directly for your sins; He takes those things you love the most."

"Do you believe this," I ask, "that your blindness is a punishment for your dad's sins?"

"Of course not. And I also did not live as a true Muslim when I was young, although my father sent us all to religious school. I became a believer at age 18, when I realized that I needed something more in my life than this society offered. Since then I have not drunk alcohol or eaten pork, and I attend mosque regularly. I met my wife at a party of Bosnians here in Hamburg. It's just easier raising children with a Muslim wife. There are no discussions about the values we want to raise them with. It's understood."

At first glance, Mahsa, an Oxford-trained British scientist, and Velija, a drummer in a local Hamburg band, might not seem to share much in common beyond their age cohort. But both are part of a new generation of European Muslims who are finding religion in ways their parents' generation had not. For these increasingly evident twenty-somethings, Islam is taking a more prominent place in their daily lives and its precepts are guiding their course. Both became devout believers as young adults: Mahsa at age 21, Velija at 18.

Velija tells me he has to avoid the temptations of male-female interactions common in European society. "There's a nice young German girl who lives in this apartment building. She often invites me in to her flat when we meet in the hallway, but I explain that I cannot. It's not right for a man to be alone with a young woman, though it's normal among most Germans. Islam is very clear on the separation of men and women. As a musician, I have close contact with female singers, dancers, and other musicians, so the temptations are difficult to avoid, but it is better to keep a respectable distance between us."

"Yes, I consider myself a fundamentalist, though that word has a different meaning to non-Muslims. You think it means terrorist. To me it just means someone who believes in the fundamentals of Islam. I believe in them and try to live by them. The temptations in this society are great."

"Of course I don't hate America," Velija says. "The problem is that Americans are so uninformed. They're the most powerful people in the world and they have the least idea of what they do abroad. My cousin lives in a small town in Pennsylvania. I called her the other week. I told her how unbelievable it is what America, which claims to support human rights, is doing to Muslims in Guantánamo [the U.S. detention center at Guantánamo Bay, Cuba]. She had no idea what I was talking about. Things that make the news everywhere else don't get discussed over there. That's one of the worst parts about your country. Your people just don't know what their country does."

Discussing 9/11, Velija makes no bones about his revulsion over what was done in the name of Islam. "Suicide is forbidden in the Quran. It's a quick ticket to Hell. One of the hijackers lived a few minutes away from here, just down the road. People who knew him said he was a friendly, sociable guy. An old lady in the neighborhood said he often helped her carry her groceries. But inside he must have been deeply troubled. Of course," Velija adds, "I wouldn't be surprised if one day we discover that the CIA had a hand in the whole affair."

This is not the first time European Muslims have told me this. The belief in a CIA or Israeli conspiracy behind 9/11 is remarkably widespread. Still, when it crops up in the middle of perfectly normal conversations, I continue to be as startled as I would be if my interlocutor had just placidly stated something akin to, "The United Nations is controlled by Neptunians."

Whatever I may think of these conspiracy theories about 9/11, the fact is that they hold sway over many European Muslims, and possibly many ethnic Europeans as well. It is a testament to just how low America's appeal has sunk. But Velija reminds me that he is of two minds regarding America. While he might believe that some Americans may have plotted to murder thousands of innocent people on 9/11, he also assigns many positive traits to the country. These include the usual litany of popular exports: music, technology, and some films. For many young Muslims, America is a land of contradictions and they are conflicted in their attitude toward it. They see some American products as wonderful, some as appalling. They see some of its values as worthy, others as repellent. The critical question for America in its effort to draw Muslim hearts and minds will be how this ambivalence is resolved.

Attracting the hearts and minds of Europe's younger Muslims is a demographic necessity. Muslim Europe is significantly younger than Christian Europe. Of France's 5 million Muslims, one-third are under 20 years old (compared to 21 percent of the French population as a whole). One-third of Germany's 4 million Muslims are under age 18 (compared to 18 percent of the German population as a whole). And a remarkable one-third of Britain's 1.6 million Muslims are under 15 (compared to 20 percent of the British population as a whole). One-third of Belgium's 364,000 Muslims are also under 15 (compared to 18 percent of the nation). Chapter 5 details the demographic trends transforming Europe.

The Islamic awakening currently underway among its younger Muslims will have a profound effect upon both Europe and transatlantic relations. The elder generations of Muslim Europe tend to be more measured in their attitudes toward America and ethnic Europeans, but a palpable shift is occurring among the young—one that presages troubled times ahead.

Malik, 29, was born in Morocco but educated in Frankfurt. He considers himself a religious Muslim and obeys Islamic principles. "America's foreign policies are shit. It's the arrogance of your country we hate most. You tell everyone you have the best democracy and that everyone else should do things your way. But your democracy is weak. True, many Arab countries are not democracies and those people don't have freedom. But you can have your ways and they have theirs. If you tell me that my food is crap and your food is best, I'll resent you. So keep your nose out of my plate."

"Have you ever been to America?" I ask.

"I dream about going to America one day."

"Wait a minute," I interrupt. "You just said you find the country arrogant and full of shitty policies. Why would you want to go there?"

"Right now, as an Arab man, I wouldn't go there. But I imagine wandering the streets of New York. I want to understand this country and this culture. Its technology and the speed of everything it produces is incredible. I can wear Reeboks and Nike clothes without accepting everything America stands for." Malik says what many Europeans say about America: it's a love-hate relationship. They are repulsed by its arrogance, its citizens' ignorance, and its policies. But they are fascinated by its power and dynamism. But for religious Muslims there are additional moral dimensions to this conflicted relationship. The wanton consumerism, the commoditization of women's bodies, the immorality shown on television and film, all create a cultural repulsion, negating much of the attractiveness from American dynamism and technological prowess.

Some of these changing values can be seen in a wide-ranging survey of more than 1,200 young Turkish-Germans. By posing a series of statements to Muslim youths and asking them to agree or disagree, Prof. Wilhelm Heitmeyer and his colleagues made some chilling discoveries. They found that despite being born and raised in Europe, pan-Islamic principles are strongly shaping young Muslims' worldviews.[3]

Pan-Islamism is rising in part because young Muslims feel excluded from European society as well as from their parents' country of birth. Forty-seven percent of Heitmeyer's young European Muslim subjects either agreed or strongly agreed with the statement, "Germans reject us, Turks in Turkey don't understand us, but Muslims accept us." Nearly one-third said that Islam must come to power in every country. Almost half believe that one should live one's life according to the Quran and reject reform and modernization of the faith and support a divine order. Fifty-six percent affirmed that even if one lives in Europe, one should not adapt too much to Western ways, but should instead live by Islam. That is the same percent as those who said that every believer must know that the religions of other nations are false and their members unbelievers. Islam is the only religion with the right beliefs. Nearly 40 percent said that Zionism, the EU, and the United States threaten Islam. Perhaps most disturbing of all, just over one-third declared that if it serves the Muslim community, then they are ready to use physical violence against non-believers.

Europe's older Muslims, the parents and grandparents who migrated here in the immediate postwar era, tend not to exhibit as strong religiosity as the youth today. In fact, Heitmeyer's findings stand in sharp contrast to an Adenauer Foundation survey of adult Turkish-Germans, which showed their attitudes remain favorable toward the German state. Ninety percent of adults said that they consider democracy the best form of government. Eighty percent claim that they are satisfied with the state of democracy in Germany, and nearly half maintained that they would defend Germany if it were attacked by Iraq or Libya—a figure higher even than among East Germans. On the other hand, one-third said that Turks are treated as second-class citizens in Germany and that their social contacts with ethnic Germans are extremely limited.

As the EU pushes forward in its drive to build a supranational identity among its more than 300 million citizens, many younger Muslims feel excluded from this project. Yet they also do not hold the same attachments to the birth countries of their parents and grandparents. A young Turk in Germany, for example, may not speak Turkish or ever have visited Turkey. He may have been born and educated in Germany, possess fluent German, and yet still not feel accepted by the society. But Muslims do accept him. At least this is what 47 percent of Heitmeyer's subjects responded when asked about their sense of group inclusion. Excluded from the pan-European identity and detached from their parents' countries of birth, they find in pan-Islamism a logical alternative.

Young Muslims across Europe are evolving distinctly different attitudes from those of their parents and grandparents. In 2003, an Ipsos survey found that while three-quarters of French Muslims believe that the tenets of Islam are compatible with the French Republic, only one-quarter of those under 25 agreed.[4]

One of Muslim Europe's prime intellectual drivers of pan-Islamism is Tariq Ramadan, grandson of Hassan Al-Banna, founder of Egypt's Muslim Brotherhood. Ramadan has taught philosophy, French literature, and Islamic studies at the University of Geneva. In 2005 he was appointed a visiting scholar at St. Antony's College at Oxford. Ramadan has become a noted expert on Islam in Europe. He is consulted by the European Parliament, has published more than twenty books, and lectures frequently across Europe and the United States. He is a member of Prime Minister Tony Blair's task force on the roots of extremism. At 43, he is captivating, thoughtful, and surprisingly controversial. He has also been denied entry into the United States under the "ideological exclusion" provision of the U.S. Patriot Act passed after 9/11.

Ramadan's case strikes at the heart of America's dilemma in the war on terror. This highly educated scholar of Western philosophy and Islamic thought preaches a message of tolerance and integration. He is the champion of the European Muslim identity, grounded in Islamic traditions and open to democratic Western ways. He is precisely the type of spokesman that America should seek to promote. In 2004, Ramadan was invited to accept a tenured position at the University of Notre Dame as Luce professor of religion at the Joan B. Kroc Institute for International Peace Studies. Only weeks before Ramadan was set to leave for the United States, the Department of Homeland Security denied his visa request. Ramadan and his family were left in limbo, with no explanation for the denial. No evidence of Ramadan's links to terrorism have been brought forth. By remaining silent on the issue, the U.S. government appears to Muslims in Europe and the United States as arbitrary and prejudiced. If a moderate Muslim scholar like Ramadan cannot even enter the United States at a university's request, then Muslims wonder who can. This type of action further erodes America's image among mainstream Muslims worldwide.

Ramadan estimates that at least 80 percent of Muslims do not practice their religion regularly or perform their daily prayers, and less than 40 percent attend the Friday mosque service. He and others, however, are quick to note the rising levels of religiosity among the youngest generation of European Muslims, those in their twenties and younger.[5] Embracing Islam is one way of defining themselves on a continent which must sometimes seem fanatically secular and from which they often feel excluded.

The sense of exclusion from European society is one factor fueling pan-Islamism among young Muslims, but another is the proliferation of satellite news programs targeted at the Muslim world. Fixated by graphic images of embattled Muslims around the world, Europe's younger Muslims increasingly identify with those perceived victims. This leads to what Graham Fuller and Ian Lesser have called a "sense of siege" within the Muslim world.[6] It is a sense that diminishes America's appeal wherever the United States is seen as opposing Muslims in global hotspots.

While Europe's younger Muslims are undergoing a type of religious awakening, Europe's Christians have been growing steadily more secular, further widening the cultural divide upon the continent. Unlike in the United States, today most nominally Christian Europeans do not attend church services and do not consider their religion as paramount in their identities. Evidence of Europe's secularity abounds, but two recent surveys put the matter in sharp relief. When asked two questions—whether they are members of a religious denomination and whether they attend services once a month or more—the results revealed a striking gap. In Britain, 83.4 percent confirmed affiliation with a particular religion, but only 18.9 percent said they attend services at least once per month or more. In Germany, 76.6 percent claimed religious affiliation, while only 30 percent attend regular services. And in France, a mere 57 percent identify with a particular religion, and an astonishingly low 12 percent say they attend services once per month or more.[7]

Church attendance is one indicator of religiosity, but notions about morality may be an even stronger measure. According to a Pew Research poll of more than 16,000 people in twenty countries in May 2003, majorities in most countries around the world, including the United States, say that it is necessary to believe in God in order to be a moral person. Europeans—both West and East—disagree, maintaining that one can be moral without God.

It is premature to declare the death of God in Europe. While Christianity has unquestionably declined in parts of Western Europe, a resurgence of religion is occurring throughout Eastern Europe, particularly in Russia. The collapse of atheistic communism and difficult living conditions may be factors in Christianity's latest renaissance. But in Western Europe, and especially in the four countries where Muslims are the most populous—Britain, France, Germany, and Holland—Christianity has suffered its severest setbacks.[8]

Incorporating large numbers of young, religious Muslims poses severe challenges to Europe's social cohesion, if not to its security. But if young Muslims are increasingly drawn to extremist messages, the dangers to domestic stability could become intense.

The gap between religious Muslims and secular ethnic Europeans is one troubling divide, but another, parallel division exists between secular and religious Muslims. This divide within Muslim Europe can be found across the continent. In Germany it is embodied in two remarkable young men: one a dynamic politician; the other a charismatic community leader. In the stories of these two men we can glimpse a sneak preview of Europe's changing identity.

Chapter 3

TWO FACES, TWO FUTURES

In the summer of 2002, normal daily life for Turks and Germans abruptly ceased. For several weeks, millions were riveted to their televisions, consumed by a high-intensity drama. At stake was nothing less than national pride and international fame. I happened to be staying in Kreuzberg, the predominantly Turkish section of Berlin, as the World Cup finals reached their quadrennial climax. On June 21, when Germany bested the United States 1-0 and advanced to the semifinals, Germany exploded in joy. Songs glorifying the German coach, Rudi Voeller, played on national radio, and beer halls across the land overflowed. Yet Kreuzberg kept curiously quiet. The following day, however, when Turkey beat Senegal, clinching its own semifinal slot, Kreuzberg erupted. For hours, car horns honked and the streets filled with jubilant crowds. Many of these Turks were born, reared, and educated in Germany. Germany was their home, and Germany was where they planned to remain. But at least as far as soccer was concerned, Germany was not where their loyalties lay.

I had come to Berlin to research Europe's Muslims. Each day I met with governmental officials and community representatives to gauge the level of Muslim integration. The official facts and figures told the story on paper. Unemployment, poverty, and crime all exceeded national averages. Surveys revealed a deep sense of Muslim alienation from European society. But the deafening roar of Kreuzberg's Turks spoke louder than any charts or statistics ever could.

Europe is caught in a quandary, and two Muslim men could not better embody it. Cem (pronounced "gem") Özdemir is a prominent Turkish-German politician, the first ethnic Turk ever elected to the Bundestag. Mustafa Yoldaş is a leading figure in Hamburg's spiritual community. Both men, in their late thirties, are ardent advocates for Muslim rights. Both are handsome, highly educated, and disarmingly charismatic. Both are first-generation Turkish-Germans, the sons of guest workers who migrated to Germany to help produce its "economic miracle," and both are devoted to changing Germany and Europe. Yet they advocate two markedly different futures for Europe's Muslims: one intensely secular, the other deeply religious.

Constant motion. I feel like I'm caught in a sudden whirlwind from the moment I pick up Cem at the Tempelhof airport in West Berlin. He has just arrived from Brussels, where his Green Party convened for a planning session. We stop by the post office to collect his mail. It's official: the notice confirming his election to the European Parliament is waiting for him. The Greens have had their best showing ever, reaching 11.9 percent of the German vote, nearly 14 percent in West Germany. There's a sense of change in the air. The Greens are on the move, and Cem is among the most popular Greens in the country, especially among younger voters, from whom Greens draw their greatest support.

In his top-floor apartment in Berlin's Moabit district, Cem's Argentine-born wife, Pia, greets us with Latin warmth. She hosts Radio Multikulti's morning music show and also anchors Deutsche Welle's Spanish-language news hour. The two have welcomed me into their home for several days, but they will keep me steadily busy.

A friend of Cem's, a cheery, openhearted young Turk, has joined us. Soon Cem's personal assistant, a 26-year-old American fluent in German, arrives as well. Several conversations are occurring simultaneously, each including Cem, who is wedded to his laptop, filling in his calendar with the latest block of appointments, meetings, and interviews. In the next few days he and I will visit Berlin's soon-to-open largest mosque, built entirely from materials sent from Turkey. He will be interviewed by a Turkish TV news station. We will eat vegetarian snacks in a local *Imbiss* (a mini-restaurant), rush back home to watch CNN's report on two bombings in Istanbul, and along the way pause in the park, where he will be interviewed by a German radio station via his cell phone. And we will crowd into a Turkish-run bar to watch the European soccer playoffs, obsessed with the outcome like nearly everyone else in Germany. Cem is a man in motion, a politician with a mission. But this isn't the life he would have predicted in his past.

Born in 1965 in the small southern German town of Bad Urach to a Turkish factory worker, Cem's birth certificate stated "Nationality: Turkish"—at that time, in Germany, outsiders could even be born inside the country.[1]

"Crazy things happened to my parents' generation when they first arrived here," Cem explains. "Here they were in a strange place, still largely unfamiliar with the language and customs. In the very beginning, some couldn't even buy a loaf of bread."

"Because of discrimination?" I ask.

"No," Cem says, "although there was plenty of that. It was because they had learned just enough German to know the phrase 'guten Morgen,' for 'good morning.' But they didn't yet know that Germans often shorten the greeting to simply 'Morgen.' But the word 'Morgen' also means tomorrow, so when some Turks entered the bakery and the clerk said 'Morgen,' the Turks thought they were telling them tomorrow, meaning 'no bread today, come back tomorrow.' The next day they returned, heard the same greeting, but they could see that the shelves were full of bread and the other customers were buying it. Then they thought that perhaps they needed to order the bread ahead of time, but they didn't know how. One man I heard about found out exactly how much a particular loaf cost so that he could rush into the bakery, put his money on the counter, grab the bread and run, before the clerk could tell him to come back tomorrow."

"There were all kinds of cultural adjustment problems," Cem continues. "My father once had to prevent a mob of angry men at the factory from beating up another Turkish worker over a simple misunderstanding. The men came to my father insisting that he speak to what they called 'one of his people.' The angry men explained that the Turkish worker was peering over the bathroom stalls, looking down at the other men as they did their business. People were shouting, calling him a disgusting pervert, and declaring that we don't do this in Germany. My father tried to calm them down and offered to talk with the alleged pervert. It turned out that he had never used a Western toilet before. Since at that time nearly all the toilets in Turkey were the kind where you squat, the man thought he had to stand with his feet on the toilet's rim. As a result, his head was raised above the stall's divider. The problem was resolved, but the German workers still thought he was a pervert, while the Turkish worker thought the Germans were barbarians since in Turkey it is considered horrendously unclean for any part of your body to touch a toilet."

Cem draws on a host of anecdotes to illustrate how little thought and planning was given to how to integrate Germany's guest workers. Clearly, the German government never intended for these guests to stay. Cem says that the hardest part for his parents' generation was that they didn't know where to be. They didn't know how long they would stay in Germany, and as time passed, they were no longer sure if they would ever return to Turkey. As a result, they could not plan.

For Cem's generation, life in Germany was equally complicated. He and hundreds of thousands like him grew up in German

schools speaking fluent and colloquial German, playing soccer
with friends, and doing all the things that teenagers do, but always
with the underlying recognition that they were not accepted as
full citizens in the only home they knew. Cem recalls a school trip
with his classmates to Belgium, where he was forced to exit the
train alone because he did not possess a visa or a German passport.
Until only recently, German citizenship was a question of blood.
If your ancestors were Germans, you were German. If not, no
amount of time in Germany, proficiency in the language, or devo-
tion to the state would matter.

The very concept of a hyphenated identity does not readily exist
in Germany, making a sense of belonging ever harder to develop.
Labels like Asian-American, African-American, or Mexican-
American, which pepper the American English vernacular, have
no equivalent in German, at least not yet. A *Turkisch-Deutscher*
(literally a Turkish-German) is not a common linguistic construction. Most Turks of this type might be called Germans of Turkish
origin, if they are not instead thought of merely as Turks living
in Germany. Cem has labeled himself an *Anatolischer Schwabe*, an
Anatolian Swabian, referring to the region of Turkey from which
his parents hail and the region of Germany in which he was born.

At 17, Cem joined the youth Green Party and quickly rose
through its ranks. He joined protest marches against the stationing
of U.S. missiles in Germany, but since he held a Turkish passport,
overt protest was risky: he could be deported if arrested. Also, by
virtue of his Turkish passport Cem was liable for service in the
Turkish military—a prospect that turned his stomach. His only
option was to renounce his Turkish citizenship and apply for German status.

Always a headache to his parents, Cem declared that he wanted
to become an *Erzieher*, or childcare worker. This is a profession
unknown in Turkey. What would his parents tell their friends?
"Our son plays with children in kindergarten for a living?" It's a
woman's profession for sure. First a vegetarian, then a protester,

then abandoning his Turkish citizenship, and now this. But Cem was to make his parents proud yet.

Often the critical turning points in a person's career are apparent only years later, but sometimes they are evident from the moment they occur. In 1993, when a series of violent attacks on Turks across German cities left several people dead, the need for ethnic Turkish representation at the federal level became clear. At the time, Chancellor Helmut Kohl, of the conservative Christian Democratic Union, infuriated Germany's Turkish residents by refusing to meet with the widow of one of those killed in the Solingen firebombings. In 2003, Chancellor Gerhardt Schröder, the liberal Social Democrat who defeated Kohl, commemorated the tenth anniversary of that ugly episode by vowing to oppose racism and xenophobia at all cost. The tone and tenor of political discourse had changed during that decade, but it did not shift on its own. The murders and subsequent weak response by the Kohl regime prompted Cem and other Turkish-Germans to elevate their political activities.

In 1994, Cem became the first ethnic Turk ever to serve in Germany's federal parliament. He recalls other parliamentarians asking him, "Herr Özdemir, are you more Turkish or more German?" One Bundestag colleague even inquired during a discussion about Turkey, "Herr Özdemir, what do *your* countrymen think?" to which he responded, "*You* are my countryman, sir."

During his tenure in the Bundestag, Cem worked to change Germany's citizenship laws to make them more inclusive. He believes that citizenship should be based not on blood, but on values; that residents' support for the constitution of the land in which they were born should be the measure of their worthiness for citizenship, not where their parents were born. As a result of pressure from the Green and Social Democratic parties, the Bundestag adopted in 2000 legislation making citizenship available to those who were born in Germany and who have at least one parent who has lived in Germany for eight years or more. Because this has not resulted in a flood of applications, critics of the new law charge that Muslims do not really want to be part of German society. But the law's proponents see other causes for the still modest response. They see it as a sign that Germany's Muslims and other non-ethnic German residents feel alienated from the society for a variety of reasons. Supporters of expanding citizenship also point to additional barriers, such as restrictions on dual citizenship. Germany requires that one renounce any other citizenship, thereby forcing Turkish-Germans to abandon any rights or privileges they might receive in Turkey. Many are reluctant to do this, especially when they do not feel accepted by their current country of residence.

Cem and I arrive at the largest mosque ever built in Berlin. It stands along a major thoroughfare and cannot be missed. The dome and minarets are striking. Nearly all of the materials used to construct it—the marble, the wood, the carpets—were imported from Turkey. Although the mosque has not officially opened for prayer, Cem and I are receiving a private tour. A Muslim graveyard lies to the right of the mosque's main entrance, where Muslims were buried more than a century before. Unlike many of the makeshift mosques I have visited across Europe—simple, small rooms that were renovated to serve a particular neighborhood—this structure is enormous. Standing in the center beneath the dome, we hear our slightest sounds echo off the walls.

We join several of the men who run the mosque for tea in the garden. We speak German, and Cem provides an occasional Turkish translation when the concepts are difficult. The first thing I ask Murat, one of the mosque leaders, is what differences he sees between the younger generation and the older.

"We organized a Turkish-German day last year," Murat tells me. "We planned a procession and passed out flags for people to carry. But the whole effort failed. The older people wanted to carry only the German flags, while the young ones would only carry Turkish flags." Cem chimes in, drawing an analogy to soccer. He tells how when he was a boy, the Turkish-German kids all wanted to play soccer, but the German teams made it difficult for them, making them play on teams for Turkish children. Today, the situation is reversed. The German government is eager to recruit young Turkish-German players, many of whom excel at the sport, but now the young boys are reluctant to join.

I notice that there are quite a few men milling about the mosque, even though it has not yet opened. Murat and the other men at our table complain about Germany's painfully high unemployment rate: more than 10 percent nationally, around 18 percent in East Germany, and as high as 30 percent in some towns and cities. Although Germany does not keep unemployment statistics based on religion, most estimate that unemployment is significantly higher among younger Muslims. "Germans have called us by three different names in the last three decades. First we were *Gastarbeiter*, guest workers. Then they called us *Auslaender*, foreigners. Now we are *Migranten*, immigrants. But in all this time little has changed for us in the workplace," complains Murat.

We start talking about America, and the first thing they mention is Israel. But they don't focus on America's policy toward Israel. Instead, they say that Israel and America are the two most arrogant powers in the world, who think they can do whatever they want and get away with it. The men say that America has even less understanding of Muslim cultures than Israel does. "We see pictures on Turkish satellite television showing American soldiers putting their feet on Iraqis. This is a terrible insult to us. I don't think your news stations even bother to show it," Murat says.

"Are there any constructive things that America can do to win over the support of more of Europe's Muslims?" I ask. A pained silence falls upon the table. Finally, one man speaks: "After Abu Ghraib," he said, referring to the widely reported abuse of prisoners by coalition forces in Iraq, "I don't think any hearts can be won."

How does Cem see the future for Germany's Muslims, who are predominantly Turkish? Cem says that he hopes they will become good German citizens who remember their Turkish heritage. He wants to see Turks in Germany develop the hyphenated identity they would have in America, retaining their Turkish language, culture, and religion, but integrating into German society, speaking fluent German, and being accepted as full German citizens. "It is simply racist to believe that democracy and Islam are incompatible," Cem says. He maintains that there is no contradiction between being a good Muslim and a good German. But Cem is admittedly secular in his own religious outlook. He also recognizes that the social problems for young Muslims are serious. He has pointed to the "sense of alienation among ethnic Turks [that] is creating conditions for a potential social explosion."

Despite the problems facing most young Muslims in Germany, life is good for Cem. He exudes optimism. He and the Greens are instruments of change. The future is rife with opportunity. By any reasonable measure, Cem Özdemir is a fully integrated European Muslim. It is possible that Cem represents more than just a constituency or a political party. He may represent the face of Muslim Europe's future: secular, young, dynamic, and open to many American ways. But at present, that future seems very much in doubt.

It's cold and wet in Hamburg. It's always cold and wet in Hamburg. And although I'm accustomed to the weather, at 8:30 am on a Sunday it feels harder to face. But Mustafa Yoldaş has no time. His medical practice is thriving, he's building a new house for his family, and his real work is never-ending.

We plan to meet in Hamburg Altona, a section in the eastern part of the city. My friend Kristine, a tall, blonde, blue-eyed East German, walks with me through the pedestrian shopping zone, which even at this hour is humming with activity. Kristine tells me she could be a foreigner in this land; everyone we see is shorter, darker, and noticeably Muslim. Most of the women are covered in headscarves.

Altona derives its name from Platt Deutsch, the last low-German dialect still spoken in Germany. Centuries ago, this part of Hamburg was occupied by the Danes. Altona is the Platt Deutsch rendering of *all zu nah*—in English, "all too near." The proximity of a foreign people made the local Germans uneasy. Ironically, today Altona is occupied by another foreign people, one that many Germans still feel is all too near.

A handshake, a warm clasp on the back. Mustafa ushers me into a bakery for tea and cakes. This is our third meeting in three years. He looks at me with his warm, round face on a closely shaved head. "Much has changed since last we met," he reports. "Every Muslim has become a suspected terrorist."

Mustafa has become one of the best-known Muslim leaders in Germany, and it's clear why. He is never short on snappy comebacks. Angela Merkel, Germany's first female chancellor, was raised in East Germany under communism, and Edmund Stoiber, a leader in Merkel's party, hails from Bavaria and speaks with a thick southern accent. "I speak better German than Stoiber," Mustafa insists, "and I've been socialized in a Western society longer than Angela Merkel, but they still don't accept me as a German."

When we first met in the summer of 2002, Mustafa was under surveillance by the German government as a suspected terrorist because of his membership in the Turkish Islamist party Milli Görüş, or National View. I asked him then why he thought the government had to tap his phone and read his correspondence. Mustafa denies ever committing any extremist acts or holding any extremist views, and he offers a stinging retort. To understand his response, you need to know that the most popular politician in the country at that time was the foreign minister, Joschka Fischer. Soon after Fischer came to power in coalition with the Social Democrats, photographs emerged showing him as one of the so-called '68ers, the generation of youth who protested against the government. In one photo, the young Fischer is shown beating a police officer. Mustafa declares, "I have never protested against

the government. I have committed no crimes nor incited anyone
to hate. But I know a man who not only protested, he violently as-
saulted the police. And what did the Germans do? They made him
foreign minister."

Not far from Hamburg's central train station, down an unin-
spiring, gritty road, stands one of Hamburg's many mosques. On
a typically cold, wet, winter evening, I visited the mosque where
Mustafa prays. This was our second encounter. Mustafa had just
begun practicing medicine, but he told me that he would not remain a full-time physician because his "heart beats more for religious issues than cardiology." This was not surprising, as his
religious activities have brought him prominence far beyond his
hometown. Mustafa has built up Hamburg's Muslim community
within an umbrella organization encompassing more than forty-
three mosques across northern Germany. One of the organization's members is the al-Quds mosque, where Mohammad Atta
and two other 9/11 hijackers once worshipped. Al-Quds allegedly
still covertly distributes videos extolling jihad and calling for action against Israel. Mustafa himself would never preach violence,
but he and many German and European Muslims do harbor grave
resentment against American foreign policy.

My visit coincided with the breaking of the Ramadan fast. After
our interview, Mustafa invited me to join the congregants, along
with several Hamburg officials and dignitaries, for the ceremonial
feast, including many homemade Turkish delicacies. As we dined,
Mustafa addressed the congregants and guests and delivered a
compelling speech on the compatibility of Islam and democracy.
Yet as I waited for the feast to begin, one congregant spoke with
me about 9/11 and speculated that either Israel or the CIA was
behind the attacks. For many Muslims, tension and resentment for
America bubble just beneath the surface.

Mustafa has argued that the war in Iraq and America's perceived
hostility to Islam have fueled resentment among growing numbers
of young Muslims. Some of these men are now heeding sermons

of violence and hate. "This is a very dangerous situation at the moment," Mustafa told the *New York Times* on April 26, 2004. "My impression is that Muslims have become more and more angry against the United States."[2]

In my most recent meeting with Mustafa, I asked him about America's image among average Muslims. "The last time we met, you said you thought Muslim resentment of America was running dangerously high. This was just after the invasion of Iraq. After more than a year of occupation, how do you think things have changed?"

Mustafa answered gravely, "I am 100 percent certain that the abuse of prisoners in Abu Ghraib won thousands, possibly tens of thousands, of sympathizers for Bin Laden. These Muslims may not actively support terror themselves, but Abu Ghraib eased the way to tacit support for terror. The tragic logic of America's actions in Iraq is that they have convinced many Muslims that America does not value their lives. They now see no reason to value American lives."

Mustafa has a litany of complaints about the worsening condition for Germany's Muslims since 9/11. An old woman calls the police merely to report that an Arabic-speaking family is living in the apartment above her. The police investigate, find nothing out of the ordinary, but the family is shaken and fearful. Police raid a Hamburg mosque in the night. The raid makes the news, but the fact that nothing was found is not reported. After Mustafa describes several such episodes, I get the point, but he continues.

Mustafa says the suspicion of Muslims and paranoia in this society is making Muslims second-class citizens. "It's a dangerous mentality that's risen again." He tells me how people complain that Muslims have not actively demonstrated against terrorism. "We have. In one protest we formed a human chain with Christian leaders and congregants, stretching from a mosque to a church. We received only three sentences in the media," Mustafa says.

Born in central Anatolia, Mustafa never had much interest in religion as a boy. In fact, his grandfather used to bribe him with money or sweets just to get him to attend the mosque. At 11 his family emigrated to Hamburg, where Mustafa quickly found himself an outsider in a strange land. But he adopted the ways of most young German teenage boys: drinking beer, eating *Wurst*, going to discos, and dating girls. But by the time he turned 18, Mustafa felt lost in this society. He found in fundamentalist Islam a peace and purpose that had been lacking.

"I might have chosen a political career, like Cem Özdemir, and I think I would have been very successful as a politician," Mustafa says. I nod. "But I chose instead to represent a community that is, to be blunt, not well loved in this country. I chose a much harder path, and I'm glad I did."

Milli Görüş, Mustafa's party and the reason he had been under surveillance, was formed in Germany in 1995 by supporters of Turkey's Islamist Refah (Welfare) Party. Refah, which strove to increase the role of Islam in Turkish politics, was eventually banned in Turkey. Its more moderate Turkish offshoot, the Justice and Development Party (AKP), is the party of Prime Minister Recep Tayyip Erdogan, who was elected in fall 2002. Although Refah has long since disbanded, Milli Görüş, its ideological heir, claims some 87,000 members across Europe, including 50,000 within Germany. Its influence is even greater than these figures suggest. It helps run roughly one-fifth of Germany's 2,500 mosques, where it distributes its literature and spreads an Islamist message. The group denies the government's charges that it supports anti-Semitism and that it wants to bring sharia law to Germany.

Frustrated by the extremist label, Milli Görüş has begun fighting back. In several court cases, the organization has challenged its opponents to prove that it is extremist. It won one case against an author, forcing him to retract erroneous allegations that the group profited from an unsavory pyramid scheme. The most high-profile case, still ongoing, involves a suit against a conservative Bremen politician who alleged that Milli Görüş proclaimed Christians among its enemies. To prove his assertion, the politician cited a Bavarian government report, which alleged that party members had made anti-Christian remarks. But Milli Görüş's 28-year-old, sharp and stylishly dressed attorney, Mustafa Yeneroglu, showed in court that the Bavarian report actually dated back to 1989, six years before the party came into being. Yeneroglu argued that it was unreasonable to ascribe any of its members' alleged remarks to the entire organization, especially when those remarks were made six years before the organization even existed.

Whatever the party's true intentions, it is exerting influence in mosques around Germany and beyond. Knowing that it will be best to have a Turkish Muslim with me as a guide to the mosques of Kreuzberg, Berlin's predominantly Turkish section, I enlist the aid of a warm-hearted man, Hasan, with a background not unlike many of Germany's East Anatolian migrants.

When Hasan was just 7 years old, a gypsy woman told him his fortune: he would travel far to distant lands and find adventure. The little boy had no idea what awaited him. Born in a tiny Anatolian village near Turkey's border with Iran, Hasan grew up in a world utterly foreign to most Europeans and Americans. His village rested atop a mountain. There was no electricity, no plumbing, no police, and for all practical purposes, no formal laws. Without access to a school, he never learned to read or write. His father raised and sold animals from village to village, while Hasan grazed the sheep.

As a young man in his early twenties, ready for the adventures the gypsy had foretold, Hasan purchased a ticket to Germany, where his uncle was working. However, this was before 1989, and he did not know there was a difference between East and West Germany. Hasan's plane landed in Schoenefeld, the airport for East Berlin.

Hasan spoke not a word of German. His uncle, who was waiting for him in West Berlin, was not there to greet him. Hasan could not operate a pay phone. He could not find anyone to translate signs for him. Even the way the toilet operated seemed inexplicable. After two days of waiting, police boarded him onto a bus for West Berlin, and a kindly German businessman saw that he was lost. That man invited him to stay in his home and work in his factory. Hasan proved industrious, and the German man and his family housed him for the next two years. Then one day, while Hasan was walking along the street, a Greek family was celebrating a birthday on a balcony above. The cork from their champagne bottle hit Hasan on the head. He looked up, smiled and waved, and the family invited him up to celebrate with them. Before long, Hasan had moved in with this family and begun working in their restaurant, where he stayed for the next four years before marrying a German woman and starting a family.

Hasan is not a fundamentalist by any means. Nonetheless, like most Muslim Europeans and many ethnic Europeans, he harbors deep concerns about America. "Your country is not a self-reflective land. Your people are so convinced of their superiority, and yet they cause so many problems around the world," Hasan says. Whatever he thinks of America the nation, he has no problems with individual Americans, and he has agreed to be my guide to some of Kreuzberg's many mosques.

We remove our shoes before entering the main prayer room of a newly renovated mosque in the heart of Kreuzberg. An elderly man in a corner is sitting on the carpeted floor, scrubbing away a little dirt, touching up the surroundings. Every mosque we enter is exceptionally clean, even the most modest of buildings. The old man tells us that every day more young people are coming to prayer times. It wasn't always that way, he adds, only in recent years has he noticed a distinct change.

In a café adjacent to one mosque, Hasan and I take a break for tea. Young men sit for hours in the afternoon, conversing in a host of languages from Arabic to Turkish to German. I am clearly an outsider, a young white man with a clean-cut, American expression. Conversations bounce back and forth like a squash ball, men at one table suddenly joining the discussion of a table across the room. I ask the Sudanese fellow next to me what he is doing in Germany. Cautiously at first, but then with greater openness, he tells me how he cannot get a visa to travel anywhere. Another man chimes in, directing his remark toward me, "We are all terrorists now." They laugh. These men have much to gripe about. Out of work and under suspicion, many feel like outsiders, even those who were born here. As for Milli Görüş, some support it, others do not, and others simply don't care.

In the antechamber outside a prayer room, I gather one of each of the fliers on display. All are in Turkish, and most are from Milli Görüş. One booklet invites potential *hajjis*—those who make the pilgrimage to Mecca—to travel with the organization for a special hajj experience. This guided group tour offers Muslims in Germany the chance to see the holiest sites in Islam through Milli Görüş's eyes.

Another flier announces a meeting to be held in a member's home to discuss the atrocities in Iraq and Palestine. It is July 2004, and Iraq is on everyone's mind. Although not directly stated, it is clear that the atrocities in question are not those of Palestinian suicide bombers or Iraqi insurgents. "Let us stand on the side of the oppressed and against oppression. Stop the violence and torture," the flier reads. "We invite anyone, man or woman, young or old, who says 'no' to the oppressing imperialists' desires." What is revealing is not that mosque-going Muslims are being called to political action, but rather the conflation of America with Israel. The two are seen as intimately intertwined, where both countries' actions in Muslim lands are viewed as comparable and oppressive. These views might not be surprising in the mosques of Cairo or Amman, but this is Berlin, the heart of Europe.

To get a better sense of Milli Görüş and its supporters in the motherland, in 2002 I had traveled to Istanbul to meet with some conservative members of the movement. My Turkish companion and I arrived at our hosts' home at 9 pm, not expecting dinner at so late an hour, but from then until 2 am, we were fed a relentless stream of Turkish cuisine, capped by three desserts served in succession. The many sweets helped to offset the sometimes bitter tensions that crackled through our conversations, especially those about America, Israel, and the Jews.

Before we arrived, my translator had warned me not to touch any of the women in this house. Handshaking with women was strictly forbidden. Even the slightest brush against the flesh would compel the woman to bathe herself fully.

Our conversation that evening began with pleasantries but quickly moved to America and Israel. While the women of the house silently prepared food in the kitchen, our host and his son-in-law offered their opinions on everything from America's role in the world to Zionist oppression of Palestinians. "We oppose Sharon, but not Israel," the host held. "It is the leadership in Israel and in America that has failed, but we have no problem with the countries themselves." Although our conversation occurred in June 2002, before America's invasion of Iraq, the resentment of American policy toward the Palestinians was evident. Like many religious Muslims, in the Middle East and in Europe, they saw America as sponsoring Israel's brutality against other Muslims, supplying the Israeli army with the tanks, missiles, and bullets that murder innocent Muslim men, women, and children. They emphasized their support for Milli Görüş in Europe as it tries to raise awareness of these connections.

In addition to all the standard complaints about American arrogance, our host also spoke heatedly about corruption within Turkey. It was evident that frustration with the previous corrupt government was widespread across the country and especially within conservative religious circles. Our host explained how the Islamist

groups he knew had been gaining support. Since state-sponsored
social services had been cut, many people had fallen into poverty.
His group collected food, clothing, medicines, and whatever es-
sentials were needed, and distributed them to the families most in
need. Here the women played a major role. His wife sometimes
went door-to-door distributing goods and talking about the importance of a government based on Islam.

"The source of all our problems is the atheists," our host declared. "We want basic human rights," he insisted, "and we hope
that the EU will guarantee them, since we don't have them now."
We spoke much about the separation of women and he quoted the
Prophet, saying that women must never be forced to do anything
but should be respected and treated fairly. "In that case," I asked,
"if your group were running a school or university, would you per-
mit female students not to wear the headscarf if they wished, and
would you defend their right not to cover?" Without hesitation
our host replied, "Of course."

It was nearly 2 am, and I had finished off the last of the desserts:
ice cream, which had followed cake, which in turn had followed
watermelon. My stomach was still groaning from the magnificent
multiple main courses they served us. I had never expected such
an elaborate welcome. Our hosts were generous to a fault. Feeling
at ease at this point, I decided to take a gamble: "Everything we
have eaten tonight has been so delicious and exquisitely prepared.
May I ask how the women in your home feel about preparing all
the meals?" Our host understood my question immediately and
accepted my challenge. "Would you like to speak with them?"

The next moment his wife and his two daughters emerged from
the kitchen and joined us in the living room. Our host invited us
to ask them any questions we wished. What followed seemed to be
a fairly open discussion, and the women expressed their content-
ment with their roles in the family and in the movement. They
spoke with pride about their hospital visits to the sick and their
food preparations and distribution to the hungry.

When our visit finally wound down, our host and his wife escorted us back to our car and thanked us profusely for listening to them. I left their home convinced of at least one thing: they are wedded to a mission, determined to translate their convictions into political action. I suspected from my other discussions in Turkey that there are many more people like them.

The next day, in conversation with a young, secular woman from Istanbul, I asked what she thought about my hosts' opinions about headscarves. While she agreed that these are clearly very kind people, she cautioned me not to accept at face value what all Islamists say. "Some insist that they will protect our right not to veil, but I don't believe it. I left my university because I had an Islamist teacher who insisted that we accept his views of Islam. He was teaching a math class, but he found a way to inject Islam into the lectures. He was definitely biased against the students who didn't share his views." Then she added, "I hope they never get control of the schools."

In November 2002, when Recep Tayyip Erdogan became prime minister in a landslide electoral victory, it sent shock and concern across Western capitals. Erdogan had once been jailed for reciting an aggressive Islamist poem in a public address. His political fortunes rebounded when AKP captured 34 percent of the national vote. It was unclear how Islamically Erdogan would rule and whether he threatened Turkey's long secular tradition. So far, Erdogan's government has acted with sophistication and diplomatic aplomb. The new government, like its recent predecessors, has been driven by a single, overriding objective: to gain Turkey's entry into the European Union. In September 2004, when the Islamists within Erdogan's government passed a law making adultery a crime, the EU immediately threatened to block Turkey's hopes of full EU membership. (Turkey has held associate membership since 1963, but progress toward equal status has taken decades.) In a rapid retreat, the penal code was quickly amended, proving the EU's power over Turkey. And precisely because the EU appears as a counter to the excesses of political Islam, many Turks in Western Europe eagerly await Turkish entry. But it is that same fear of political Islam that in part is slowing the membership process.

It's a Saturday night, and I am walking through Halle's center city. The restaurants are not full; even the pubs are quiet. The streets are almost empty, and I am conscious of the sound of my own footsteps. For a city of more than 240,000, the city seems eerily still.

Capital of the East German state of Saxon-Anhalt, Halle has played an important part in German economic and cultural history. Long known for its salt production (the town's name derives from the Celtic word for salt), the city later developed a potent chemical industry. In the town center stands a statue of famed Baroque composer, Georg Friedrich Händel, who was born here. The composer Wilhelm Friedemann Bach spent eighteen years as a church organist here. In the eighteenth century, Halle was central to the spreading of Lutheranism abroad, sending missionaries to the United States. Henry Melchior Muhlenberg, a Halle native and patriarch of the Lutheran Church in America, has a college in Pennsylvania named for him, and his son, Frederick Augustus Muhlenberg, a graduate of Halle University, served as America's first Speaker of the House of Representatives. In 1990, Halle had a population of some 311,000, but the economic malaise that has depressed East Germany since unification has led to mass migration westward. Census figures for 2001 put the population at 240,000. Official national unemployment in Germany hovers around 12 percent, but in East Germany it runs as high as 20 percent, and some believe that these official figures are underestimations. Whatever the actual unemployment rate in Halle may be, I cannot help sensing an undercurrent of anger from many of the locals, even in the simplest of exchanges. I am clearly a foreigner, and so is Esma Mutlu.

Esma moved to Halle from Istanbul nine years ago to join her husband, Mehmet, who had found work in construction. "I couldn't speak German," Esma says, "and because there were so few Turks here, it was lonely and isolating, but that forced me to learn the language fast." Today, she speaks fluent German. She works in a pharmacy, having earned the requisite credentials. Yet she does not feel part of German society. "I still feel like I'm treated as a foreigner, despite that I work here, pay taxes, and have legal residency."

"I think the East Germans just never had much contact with foreigners, so it was hard for them and for us," Esma continues. "I am still very careful during night hours and try to avoid some parts of our town even during the daytime."

Esma and Mehmet welcomed me into their apartment for the weekend, showed me their town, took me to Leipzig for a tour, and, as was true of every Muslim I have met in my travels across the continent, hosted me with the greatest possible hospitality. They even drove me back to Berlin (the nearest place they can get Turkish food) and treated me to dinner at their favorite Turkish restaurant in Kreuzberg.

As for her faith, Esma says it is important to her, though like many Turks from cosmopolitan cities such as Istanbul and Ankara, she is not a fundamentalist, she opposes the wearing of headscarves in public schools, and she believes Turkey rightfully belongs in the EU. "I wish Turkey could be an EU country because my life would be much easier. I could transfer all of my college credits, I would be able to drive with my Turkish driving license. These are some personal reasons, but I also think Turkey can profit from membership economically and culturally. We already have the signed 1963 agreement making Turkey an associate member and the application for full membership. I think it is time to keep the promises which were made forty years ago." Esma's wishes notwithstanding, Turkey's EU membership will not come easily, primarily because including a Muslim nation into the EU will fundamentally and irrevocably alter Europe's identity.

Germany's conservative party, the Christian Democratic Union, has led the opposition to Turkish membership, and the bloc of Christian Democratic parties within the European Parliament echoes their view. Back in 1998, the Belgian Wilfried Martens, leader of the EP's European People's Party, called Turkey's candidacy "unacceptable."[3] While they supported cooperation with Turkey, he explained, they opposed membership because, "the European project is a civilisational project." In other words, the political right saw Turkey as belonging to a separate, non-European civilization. I heard this view expressed more explicitly at an academic conference on the future of "the West" that I attended in 2004, in Philadelphia. One British gentleman asked a speaker —and though I am paraphrasing his remarks based on memory, the meaning is certain—"Why do you Americans insist on pressing us to admit Turkey into the EU? Turkey is an alien nation to Europe. It is as if we told America to airlift Zambia and append it to the United States." Martens and the other right-of-center opponents of Turkish membership have since been overruled.

In December 2004, the die was officially cast. After decades of stalling and debate, the EU at last decided to begin talks with Turkey about its path toward EU membership. The decision is peppered with caveats and hedges. Nevertheless, it binds the EU to consider uniting with a country that by the time accession is possible (roughly 2020) would be the largest nation in the Union, with a population of some 80 million Muslims. Whichever way the EU member states decide, their decision will have an unimaginable impact on the millions of Muslims already living within EU borders. The question is whether Muslims can and will be genuinely included in the construction of a European identity.

Europe is still struggling to devise a coherent strategy for integrating its Muslim residents. Spain's dynamic young prime minister, José Luis Rodríguez Zapatero, has called for a "cultural alliance" between the West and the Muslim world, an all-encompassing forum to explore everything from interfaith dialogues to joint peacekeeping missions. French Labor Minister Jean-Louis Borloo is touting a "Marshall Plan" for towns, a $12.7 billion program to create jobs and combat poverty in the mainly Muslim ghettos outside Paris, Marseilles, and Lyon. Tony Blair's government is constructing a "hearts and minds campaign" to support moderate imams while expelling radical ones. It is too early to say whether any of these grand schemes will bear fruit, but strategic planning has yet to reach the EU level. Much is riding on the outcome. If they succeed, Europe's Muslims could serve as a crucial bridge to the rest of the Islamic world. The more that young Muslims feel themselves a part of European society, equal members of a true EU, the less that radical alternatives will be appealing. But if these programs fail, the result will be domestic fragmentation, social unrest, and potentially violent religious extremism.

Europe faces two distinctly different, equally plausible futures. One embraces Muslims as part of the new European identity. The other excludes moderate, religious Muslims, leaving them prey to the call of Islamic extremists. Both Cem and Mustafa are working toward the former, a European identity inclusive of secular and religious Muslims, though their means to that end are distinct. The obstacles before them are considerable. Speaking about Germany, Mustafa says that Muslims are now living as second-class citizens. If the darker future results, and Muslims feel excluded from the Europe they call home, the repercussions will be profound. Even the optimistic Cem says that the conditions are ripe for a social explosion. If the Madrid and London bombings and their violent backlash are not to become the norm across the continent, Europe must soon solve its Muslim quandary. Europe's, and America's, security depends on it.

Chapter 4

HEADSCARF HEADACHES,
CARTOON CHAOS

"We have gone to war against the multicultural ideology that says that everything is equally valid," declared Brian Mikkelsen, the Danish minister of cultural affairs, in a speech at his party's annual convention. "The culture war has now been raging for some years. And I think we can conclude that the first round has been won." The next front, he said, is the war against the acceptance of Muslim norms and ways of thought.[1]

Hindsight, they say, is always 20/20, yet even after the protests erupted, the Danish government still seemed remarkably unaware of the damage it had wrought. On October 12, 2005, eleven ambassadors from Muslim states to Denmark requested an official meeting with the government to discuss the twelve inflammatory political cartoons published in the regional newspaper *Jyllands-Posten*. The illustrations depicted the Prophet Mohammed and other scenes suggesting that Muslims are terrorists. The government refused to meet with the ambassadors, only backing down at last on February 3, 2006, one week after boycotts of Danish products had begun and the protests had turned violent. By then, it was too late. Kashmir urged a general strike to protest the cartoons, Iran initiated a cartoon mockery of the Holocaust, and the Dan-

71

ish embassy in Beirut was burned—one man died in the incident. As with the upheaval that engulfed Holland following Theo van Gogh's murder little more than a year before and the car burnings that convulsed France the previous November, Europeans and Americans now watched in puzzlement and fear as Muslims vented their anger at European insensitivity. Some insisted it was a matter of free speech. Twelve renowned writers, Salman Rushdie and Ayaan Hirsi Ali among them, published a manifesto calling Islamism the new fascism.[2] Others felt that the newspapers had disrespected Islam and Muslims. Herbert Pundik, the former editor-in-chief of Denmark's *Politiken* newspaper, argued that the major papers should take up a collection to fund a mosque in Copenhagen, replete with minaret and dome, as a means of atoning for the country's poor treatment of its Muslim population. Pundik was once among the Jews ferried to safety by Danes while the Nazis pursued.

Like few issues before it, the cartoon controversy painfully illustrated the culture clash at play across the continent. Once more, the issue came down to values: free speech versus religious tolerance. It later emerged that the editor of *Jyllands-Posten* had three years earlier refused to publish cartoons of Jesus which he deemed offensive to Christians. Understandably, many Muslims viewed this as a typical European double standard. While free speech is critical to a democracy, one of freedom's responsibilities is surely to show respect for the beliefs of others. European insensitivity over the cartoons may have contributed to breeding future Bin Ladens, but the overwhelming majority of Europe's Muslims objected peacefully to the affair. One Muslim man even resorted to comedy.

Omar Marzouk is a 32-year-old Danish-Muslim comic. The son of Egyptian immigrants, Marzouk abandoned the computer company he founded to turn his talents to getting laughs. In his one-man show, "War, Terror, and Other Fun Stuff," Marzouk tells audiences of his plan to counter terrorism and reduce Muslim unemployment simultaneously. Marzouk suggests that governments hire Muslims to sit on buses while strapped with explosives. That way, when a real suicide bomber gets on, they can say, "Hey, man, it's OK, I got this one covered." Marzouk believes that the decision to publish the Danish cartoons was intended to offend Muslims, but he does not want to see a restriction on free speech, since he recognizes that the same openness to expression enables him to poke fun at whatever he likes. He says he doesn't worry when performing if his jokes bomb, because if they do, "they go straight to heaven where they get 72 virgin jokes."[3]

The cartoon affair should have served two critical functions: to underscore the need to balance free speech against respect for religious sensitivities and to reinforce the fact that Islamic extremists do exist inside Europe and must be countered. Few outside of Denmark realized that the cartoon of Mohammed wearing a turban with a bomb inside bore the likeness of Sheikh Abu Laban, one of Copenhagen's more radical Muslim clerics. A political refugee in Denmark since 1984, Abu Laban has called for the return of the caliphate in Arab lands and suggests that eventually enough converts could exist to bring Europe under the caliphate as well. It is views such as these that stir European fears.

Why does so much anger surround the publication of a few offensive cartoons? The answer is that both sides fear the larger assault on their identity that the issue evokes. The cartoons compel European Muslims to ask: how can we coexist in a European society that disrespects our practices and belittles our faith? Non-Muslim ethnic Europeans wonder the inverse: can Europe preserve its identity in the face of such zealots as Abu Laban, and how will the spread of Islam across the continent alter the European identity? Identity politics and the fears that infuse them are what charge debates over such seemingly innocuous issues as the publication of cartoons or the wearing of headscarves by schoolgirls.

Scarf vs. State

After a long political exile in Germany, a young Turkish poet returns to the remote city in Eastern Turkey where he had studied years before. He is drawn by a morbid curiosity, he claims, to discover why teenage girls have been committing suicide after they are forbidden to wear their headscarves in school. Having only just arrived, he inadvertently witnesses the brutal shooting of the school's director who had enforced the ban. The assassin had been sent to destroy the infidels who, as he saw it, wished to force young women into exposing themselves, disgracing their honor and desecrating Islam. When a terrible snowstorm seals the city off from his familiar Western world, the poet finds himself drawn into the Islamists' underworld, where his beliefs and his life are at risk.

This is the premise of Orhan Pamuk's best-selling novel, *Snow*, and though the story is pure fiction, it graphically depicts the very real divide within Turkey: that between devout Islamists on the one hand and secular, Western-looking Turks on the other. In Turkey, the balance, for now, remains in favor of the secularists, backed by the military. As mentioned in chapter 3, the lure of entry into the European Union is also keeping Islamist tendencies at bay. But the headscarf debate still percolates just below the surface of Turkish politics. One day in May 1999, it brought the nation to a near breaking point.

Merve Kavakçi entered the Parliament chamber with her head held high. She had been democratically elected to serve her constituency. Yet for roughly forty minutes after entering, her colleagues kept up a steady stream of shouts for her to leave. "Get out! Get out!" the legislators cried. Finally, the prime minister, Bülent Ecevit, raised his hand, pointed at Kavakçi, and exclaimed, "Put this woman in her place!"

What had Kavakçi done to cause such a fracas? She was the first female parliamentarian to wear the hijab, the Muslim headscarf and veil. Under Turkish law, headscarves are banned for public officials. Turkish authorities see it as a symbol of political extremism, incompatible with the secular state they have sought to build since the Republic's founding by Kemel Atatürk in 1923. But Kavakçi saw it as a matter of religious conviction. Reflecting on the experience five years later, Kavakçi explained that although some women are forced to veil, many do it freely. Calling the oppression myth a common Western misconception, she wrote, "For women who choose it, the headscarf is an indispensable part of their personal identity, one that should not be compromised. If Western feminists and other critics want to advance women's rights, they are better off honoring a woman's right to choose rather than trying to impose their prejudices on Muslims."[4]

Once, heated headscarf incidents were only a Turkish problem. Today, the matter has spread across Europe. And for Muslims already living within the EU, where no military sticks or EU-membership carrots hold any sway, the stakes are even higher.

Fereshta Ludin was just doing her job. At least, that's how she saw it. But when Ludin, a German schoolteacher of Afghan origin, declined to remove her headscarf in the classroom, school authorities demanded the head covering be removed. When she refused, the authorities sacked her.

Ludin's case found its way to the German Supreme Court. After much consideration, the ruling handed down by the Court was far from definitive. Although it declared it illegal to prevent teachers from wearing the veil, it simultaneously permitted German states to make their own rulings on the issue. In other words, it passed the buck back to the states. Four states immediately declared that they would enact headscarf bans, including Ludin's own state of Baden-Wurtemberg. More recently, in January 2005, the Danish Supreme Court ruled that a 27-year-old grocery store clerk could not wear her veil to work because the company's uniform did not include the hijab. While the headscarf debate continues to rage across Europe, nowhere has the matter been more heated than in France.

In December 2003, the U.S. State Department released its annual religious freedom report to Congress. According to law, the State Department is required to review and assess the degree of religious freedom afforded to peoples in every country. This is the report which typically rounds up the usual suspects—China, Burma, Sudan, and company—and rebukes them for not providing a more tolerant atmosphere to minority religious groups. But that year the American ambassador-at-large for religious freedom, John Hanford, added France to the blacklist. Earlier that same week, President Chirac, after hearing the report from an investigative committee he established, decided to ban all prominent religious symbols from public schools. A few months later, on March 15, 2004, France's legislature made the ban official. The ban includes visible Catholic crosses and Jewish skullcaps, but its true target is the hijab. When the ban was made law, thousands of Muslim women flooded the streets of France to protest it. What they want, they say, is not to have all symbols banned, but to have all religious symbols welcomed.

France's headscarf headaches date back more than a decade. A 1989 survey revealed that 75 percent of French citizens opposed the wearing of veils in schools, with 17 percent indifferent, and only 6 percent in favor. Today, with Islamophobia rising across the continent, reactions have grown even more intense.

France is founded on principles of separation of church and state. The wearing of religious symbols in public places, officials insist, threatens this fundamental value. Until Chirac's recent ban on all religious symbols, Catholic students were permitted to wear crosses and Jews their yarmulkes. This differential treatment was never lost on France's Muslims. To many French Muslims, the previous state policy seemed both hypocritically anti-Muslim and unwisely backward in its effects on Muslim women. But Chirac's ban did not remedy the situation.

The common perception is that the veil's increasing prevalence signifies a rise in Islamic extremism, making the scarf an enticing target for those who feel France's traditional culture is under siege. Yet rarely do the headscarf opponents ask what motives lie behind the veil. Rather than reflecting a rise in militancy, Muslim women choose to veil for a host of reasons.

Some wear the hijab to appear righteous and pure, thereby gaining respect within their local community. Other women find the hijab, unlike revealing Western dress, a coat of armor, shielding them from the jeering comments and sexual harassment which sometimes comes from men in public places. Others use it as a fashion statement. In fact, enough French Muslims wear colorful designer headscarves that instead of being called by its actual name "tchador," some have nicknamed it a "tcha*dior*," after the famous designer, Christian Dior.

Beyond these reasons, many younger Muslim women say that the hijab forces men to respect them for their intellect and abilities, not their looks. Sajida Madni, a 23-year-old teacher in Birmingham, put it this way. "Many friends find comfort in the hijab because they feel it frees them. I mean that things have got out of hand these days—women are pressured into feeling they have to look glamorous to be noticed in a man's world."[5]

In a fascinating study of working-class women in Cairo—a study which may have direct relevance to European Muslims—Prof. Arlene MacLeod of Bates College shows that many women who had previously not veiled are now choosing to wear the hijab.[6] Economic pressures are one factor driving their decision. With the high cost of living, both husband and wife usually need to earn income. However, women are typically still solely responsible for the household affairs (cooking, cleaning, and child care). Women complain that their husbands do not appreciate the demands on their time. The husbands disparage them for not having meals ready on time or having their shirts neatly ironed. Women's traditional roles as wife and mother have now merged with the role of income earner, but no modern identities have supplanted the old ones. That's where the hijab comes in.

Many of these women, MacLeod finds, have chosen to wear the veil as a means of gaining respect, both from their husbands and their communities. The moment they don the headscarf, they are suddenly seen as good, pious Muslims. The veil represents the traditional values of honor, virtue, dignity, competence in the home, and of course, modesty. The hijab also prevents men from discussing their bodies, treating them as sexual objects, or commenting about their appearance in the streets on their way to work.

The headscarf, veil, and traditional Muslim dress afford women a means of resisting the objectionable treatment from men in their own culture. MacLeod has dubbed this re-veiling trend "accommodating protest" because she sees it as both a form of resistance to domination and a simultaneous acquiescence to men's behavior. Rather than demanding that men alter their disrespectful behavior, women have adjusted their own reactions to it.

Remember Oona King, the British MP from chapter 1, who lost her seat in Parliament over the Iraq war? King once admitted that she was surprised to find burkas in Bethnal Green, the district she represented. When America liberated Afghanistan from Taliban rule, many believed that women would now be free to shed their oppressive burkas, the long, concealing dress that Taliban leaders compelled all women to wear. To the surprise of some observers, many Afghan women have continued to wear their burkas, not out of oppression from governmental officials or husbands, but out of choice, seeing it as part of their culture and religious beliefs. When King encountered burkas in her own backyard, she said "the scales sort of fell from my eyes." King, a noted feminist and former assistant to the British Minister for Women, had previously seen burkas as a sign of oppression. Once she understood that some women cover themselves voluntarily, she said she would defend the right of any of her constituents to wear a burka, though not in schools, since teachers must be able to see their students' faces. "But if they're over 18 and not in school, certainly," King confessed. "It's their choice."[7]

Of course, there are those who are forced to veil by their husbands and fathers. For schoolgirls like these, veiling is often their only option if they don't want their parents to forbid them from attending mixed-gender classes. In such cases French and German policy could prevent many girls from obtaining an education, inhibiting their later integration into European society.

There is, however, another wrinkle to this story. The nineteen members of Chirac's commission received testimonies from Muslim girls and their parents requesting that the ban be imposed. The reason involved tremendous peer pressure. In schools where some Muslim girls wore the hijab and others did not, the unveiled girls often bore the verbal insults and threats of Muslim boys. These fundamentalist boys called the unveiled girls "whores" and in some cases physically attacked the girls. Some Muslim parents had transferred their daughters to private Catholic schools in order to escape the pressure from fundamentalists. Then the situation worsened. Because denouncing other Muslims is sometimes seen as a treasonous act within communities, girls who had had their arms broken or suffered other forms of attack, lied to their parents and school authorities to protect the perpetrators. The Presidential Commission realized that by allowing individual school principals to determine whether the hijab should be banned, this would enable radical fundamentalists to target and intimidate those principals who enforced the ban. The Commission feared that extremists would be emboldened, and principals—like the unfortunate victim in Pamuk's novel—could be at risk. The Commission saw the headscarf issue not just as a matter of personal freedom to choose one's dress code. Instead, they saw it as part of a larger struggle against a rising, aggressive Islamic fundamentalism.

This battle is almost certainly not over. The French state demands control over education, but the Islamists are intent on wresting some control for themselves. It is no accident that so much intensity revolves around a schoolroom. Education is the mechanism for a modern state's influence over the national identity. The great German thinker Max Weber famously argued that the modern state must control the means of violence (the military, a police force, and other instruments of physical coercion) in order to maintain its power. But making an implicit reference to Weber, the scholar Ernest Gellner updated Weber's maxim, asserting that, "The monopoly of legitimate education is now more important, more central, than is the monopoly of legitimate violence."[8]

As divisive as the headscarf has been between ethnic Europeans and their Muslim residents, it has at times been even more divisive within the Muslim community. The testimony that Chirac's Commission received is but a small part of the violence which too often infuses life for young French Muslim women. Samira Bellil was only 13 when she experienced her first rape. She was living in one of the Paris suburbs that have become Muslim ghettos. Samira did not wear the hijab, but Western clothes. In the depressed suburbs, she was an easy target of male aggression. Admiring a boy who led a local gang and wanting to be liked, Samira became a *fille à cave*, or "cellar girl." Cellar girls are young women who are repeatedly gang-raped, shared by men as Samira put it, in the same way as CDs you would loan to a friend. She was frequently beaten badly and found little chance of escape.[9]

Samira's case is not unique. Many of the Muslim suburbs around France's major cities are experiencing rising incidents of rape. Furious at the lack of support from French police and outraged at the government's apparent lack of concern, several young rape victims have formed organizations to draw public attention to the problem. The *Ni Putes, Ni Soumises* (roughly translated, "neither whores nor servants") movement has gained national attention for this cause, displaying enormous posters of rape victims on Bastille Day in Paris.[10] Young women such as these feel that if they must cover themselves just to avoid rape and harassment, then the hijab is very much a symbol of oppression.

After conducting in-depth interviews with French Muslim women of North African roots, Emory University sociologist Caitlin Killian found the same divided opinion over headscarves.[11] Most of France's nearly 5 million Muslims either themselves emigrated from the Maghreb ("the West" in Arabic, the region of North Africa including Algeria, Tunisia, and Morocco) or are the offspring of Maghrebians. While many of her interview subjects who favored the veil did not veil for political reasons, there were other Muslim women who opposed the hijab on political grounds. These Muslim women believe that the goal of French schooling is to enable integration, and they see the veil as a clear impediment. Amel, a 26-year-old Algerian woman, objected to the veil this way: "For me it's a choice to make. You study and you go to a secular school, meaning you respect the laws, no exterior signs, or otherwise you stay at home. And the veil she can wear it from morning until night, nobody will stop her."

A few of those Killian interviewed expressed genuine anger at those Muslims who do not adapt. This attitude is most harshly articulated by Lina, a 32-year-old Algerian who experienced oppression in Algeria. "Buddy, you want to live like that, go back to your village. Go back. You are not made to live here. . . . Why do you take the good things from France and why do you try to bother people, send your daughter to school with the veil, piss off the people around you?" Hyat, another 32-year-old Algerian, who herself had strict parents, remarked: "These girls, there are parents who prefer to keep them home rather than let them go out without the veil. So imagine all the damage you're doing to that young girl. You're destroying her future. You have to see this humanitarian side, to see that actually they are victims. You can't destroy the future of these girls."

Killian also discovered that most North African French-Muslims have not sought French citizenship. Although they could obtain citizenship after five years of permanent residence, only one-third of Tunisian immigrants and a mere 15 percent of Algerian and Moroccan immigrants have acquired it. This low citizenship rate may reflect, as in Germany, a sense of alienation or exclusion from mainstream French society. If it does, then the headscarf ban would only exacerbate that sense and further hinder integration.

Opposition to the headscarf ban has been voiced in varied quarters, from Shirin Ebadi (the Iranian human rights advocate who won the Nobel Peace Prize) to Pope John Paul II, who warned that religious freedom in Europe was in danger. Reflecting on Germany's Supreme Court verdict in the Fereshta Ludin case, the country's then president, Johannes Rau, questioned the ban's wisdom. "If one bans the headscarf in schools as a religious symbol, it is difficult to defend the monk's habit." Rau continued, "Our constitution requires equal treatment of religions in the public sphere—including schools. That does not put our Christian heritage in question."[12] President Rau is right. Banning symbols like headscarves furthers the mistaken view that these symbols solely represent political extremism and misses the complex and varied meanings behind the veil. It also sends a negative message to young women. Mustafa Yoldaş, the Muslim leader in Hamburg profiled in chapter 3, told me that his own teenage daughter was thinking about becoming a teacher. After the ban, however, she had second thoughts. "I think it's terrible," Mustafa said, "that a child's dreams have to be limited just because of discrimination."

Mustafa had a point, and I could not resist noting that in America, Muslims are free to wear the hijab in school, at work, or wherever they like. In fact, in the fall of 2004, 18-year-old Emily Smith, a high-school student in Tennessee, was told that she could not wear her headscarf in school. A few days later, the Council on American-Islamic Relations wrote the superintendent on Emily's behalf. CAIR explained that Emily's right to cover her head is protected by the Constitution. After consulting with its lawyers, the school district swiftly reversed its decision. Mustafa admitted that he wished Europe would adopt America's approach to this issue.

At the root of Europe's headscarf headaches lies the fear of Muslim extremism, but laying siege to a symbol will not secure the state, especially when that symbol does not always reflect the extremism it hopes to ban. Rather than banning all religious symbols as a means of excluding the Muslim garb, a wiser policy would be to include the hijab among acceptable symbols, while simultaneously cracking down on Islamists who try to compel women to cover. This would do more to incorporate Muslims into European society, reducing everyone's sense of siege. But fixating on the scarf only shrouds the deeper problems from view.

Culture Clash

What is the proper way to beat your wife? Not at all. At least, that's how a Spanish court saw it in January 2004, when it sentenced imam Mohamed Kamal Mustafa to fifteen months in prison for authoring a book on the proper technique for disciplining one's wife. To his credit, the imam did recommend not striking the woman on sensitive body parts but instead restricting the beatings to the hands and feet with the use of a light rod or cane. The Spanish judge declared that Kamal's book was "infused with a tone of obsolete machismo," and "incompatible with the reigning social mores."[13]

Mustafa's case is not unique. In 2004, Amsterdam's El Tawheed mosque came under intense scrutiny when it was found to be selling a book entitled *The Way of the Muslim*, which called for the defenestration of homosexuals. If the gay person is not dead upon hitting the ground, the book explained, then the homosexual should be stoned to death. The mosque had previously sold a book encouraging female genital circumcision and wife-beating. Spain and Holland are not alone. In April 2004, a French court deported a 52-year-old imam to Algeria for condoning both wife-beating and stoning for improper behavior. Abdelkader Bouziane preached that the Quran permits wife-beating in cases of infidelity. The French court would have none of it. Dominique de Villepin, at that time France's Interior Minister, intervened personally in the case, ordering Bouziane's immediate expulsion. In his defense, Bouziane's lawyers argued that it would be unfair to separate the imam from his sixteen children and both of his wives.[14]

Technically, Islam permits men to have up to four wives. Occasionally reports surface in Europe of Muslim men taking one wife under law, and another through a Muslim ceremony which is not legally recognized. Tariq, a 56-year-old British Muslim, explained his decision this way. "I did not wake up in the morning and think 'I'll get married again to someone younger or more sexy.' I had to have a special reason." Tariq's reason was that Tasmin had divorced her first husband after he beat her. She was struggling to make ends meet by working in a London post office and raising her two children. Tariq offered her a job with his film production company, and their relationship developed. Tariq's first wife agreed to his taking the second wife, and although the two women live in separate homes, all three regularly meet to discuss family business.[15] Ostensibly, it works for them, but it is certainly not the standard British way.

Traditional Muslim practices are increasingly conflicting with European social values. Often these conflicts revolve around women and questions of how their bodies should be treated. The problems are intensified when Muslim women themselves insist on practices which European women oppose. Unfortunately, many of these practices are not condoned by Islam; they are merely cultural traditions that some Muslims from non-Western countries still observe.

A Danish Success

"We had absolutely no idea how to deal with it. Our health care workers were completely unprepared." Dr. Viebecke Jorgensen slides a plate of freshly baked Danish pastries across the table and pours me a cup of tea. Spotting my expression of surprise and discomfort, she adds, "We had simply never encountered it before."

We sit in her home in a posh Copenhagen suburb, chatting in the sunroom, though the rain continues to drizzle outside. Dr. Jorgensen, a stately, well-spoken advocate, headed the Danish Women's Medical Association for twenty years. Although she retired in 1993, she remains active on the issue that has consumed her for several decades: female genital mutilation (FGM). In fact, she has just returned from Brussels, where she helped found a European-wide organization to combat the scourge afflicting too many of Europe's young Muslim women.

FGM is still commonly practiced in a few Muslim countries.[16] It is estimated that 98 percent of Somali girls were circumcised between 1992 and 1993, and the percentage may remain that high today, although accurate figures are difficult to obtain. The procedure is usually performed on girls between the ages of four and fourteen by someone holding them down, spreading their legs, and taking a knife, scissors, razor blade, tin lid, or broken glass and partially or wholly cutting away the clitoris. Because the practitioners are typically female village elders whose eyesight is often failing, they sometimes do even more damage than expected.

The initial complications of FGM include severe pain, urine retention, shock, hemorrhaging, and infection, with the latter two symptoms sometimes proving fatal. The long-term effects include cysts, abscesses, scarring, damage to the urethra, difficulties with childbirth, and sexual dysfunction. But the psychological impact is impossible to measure. The experience itself can be terrifying.

A host of myths have enabled FGM to continue within certain African Muslim communities. These include the belief that it promotes cleanliness and virginity. Without a functioning clitoris, it is believed, a woman will not seek sexual activity. Many think that Islam mandates the act, though the Quran is silent on the matter. Other myths include a fear that a child will die in childbirth or a man will die during intercourse if an uncircumcised clitoris is touched. "The death in childbirth myth may have arisen," Jorgensen suggests, "because many Somali and West African girls give birth at such young ages, before their pelvises are sufficiently mature. This can cause complications during childbirth, sometimes death." Still others maintain that the uncircumcised genitals will grow large and hang between a woman's legs, and that the food she cooks will smell bad. Such legends sound absurd, but it is unwise to underestimate the power of legend in any society, traditional or modern.[17]

Between 100 and 140 million girls and women around the world are estimated to have undergone FGM, with cases being reported in Britain, France, Holland, Denmark, Sweden, and the United States. FGM is illegal in all of these countries, yet the practice persists. According to French Penal Code Article 222-9, acts of violence resulting in mutilation or permanent disability are punishable by up to ten years' imprisonment and a fine of 150,000 euros. If mutilation is performed on a minor (under age 15), the maximum imprisonment is increased to fifteen years.

France's harsh penalties stand in contrast to Denmark's softer approach. FGM was certainly not something the Danes ever expected to see in Copenhagen's emergency rooms. But when civil war in Somalia led some 14,500 Somalis to seek shelter in the tiny Danish homeland, soon Danish physicians began seeing cases of FGM and its painful aftermath. Determined to arrest the trend, the Danish minister of health formed a working group of medical practitioners and public health officials to change attitudes among Somali residents. The Danes believed that it would be more effective to attack the root problem, Muslim attitudes, than simply to prosecute the perpetrators themselves. In 1997, a working group within the National Board of Health began speaking with Somali community leaders and Muslim parents directly. They convened a group of imams to discuss the subject, and the imams concluded that female circumcision is not a religious duty. The working group created a video in the Somali language, in which Somali community leaders explain that the practice is illegal, that it poses serious health risks, and that it is contrary to Islam.

The Danish approach appears to be succeeding. Awareness among Danish Somalis is up, incidents of FGM are down, and community relations improved. There may be a lesson in Denmark's experience, one that holds hope for Muslim integration across Europe. Harsh penalties may not deter these kinds of practices; they may only deter the victims from seeking help. It may be wiser for the European governments to invest in changing attitudes. Until they do, conflicts are bound to continue and intensify.

The Danish experience reveals another fault line in Muslim Europe's tenuous efforts to integrate into European society. Although FGM is not an Islamic practice, because some African Muslims still observe it, it has become associated with Islam in the public mind. Even the Ethiopian Jews have been known to practice FGM, despite their strict adherence to Old Testament laws. There is no mention of FGM in the Old Testament, but local African traditions became incorporated into these Jews' customs.[18] FGM has not been associated with Judaism in the European public's mind. But where Muslims represent a small and relatively recent presence in a European state, the opportunities for misconceptions are extremely high. Negative public attitudes then reinforce what are already distressing social ills.

The Expert's Bottom Line

Somalis, and Muslims more generally, do not enjoy a positive image in many Danes' minds. The anti-Muslim hate crimes that have swept across Europe have touched even Denmark's traditionally tolerant society. In January 2005, vandals desecrated some 100 Muslim grave markers in Copenhagen's Vestre Kierkegaard cemetery. When I heard about acts like this I wanted to hear from an expert what he thought was the cause for this peaceful, socially progressive country's Muslim dilemma. It was time to see Torben Svendrup, a scholar with IND-sam, the Association of Ethnic Minorities.

It's a rainy, summer afternoon on the University of Copenhagen campus. Svendrup lights yet another cigarette, takes a gulp of
coffee, and leans across the cafeteria table at me. Trained as a historian, Svendrup wears his academic role like his well-worn suit.
In his late fifties, he is ebullient, engaging, and does not mince
words.

"Why are Muslim crime and unemployment rates so high in
Denmark?" I ask. "I'll tell you why," Svendrup replies. "When you
get sick, you probably know some doctors you can call at home,
don't you?" He points his cigarette at me accusingly. I nod. "And
when you need legal advice, you probably have some lawyers you
can contact—friends, or friends of friends, or family relations.
Don't you?" The cigarette is jabbing in my direction. "It's true," I
admit. "And when you need a job, a decent job with a respectable
salary, you have a whole network you can at least access to get you
started on the search, don't you? It's social capital, and Muslims
have none of it."

Svendrup chaired a commission for the former Social Democratic government to study the country's Muslims. "I work for
no government," he corrects me. "I am a human who works for
science." I stand corrected. But Svendrup does assist the Danish
government by researching Muslim social issues in depth. He says
the unemployment rate among Somalis is over 70 percent, a figure that seems almost inconceivable given Denmark's generous
social infrastructure. But the random Danes I speak with reveal
the same concerns. They see many Muslims as lazy, irresponsible,
or as criminals.

Three cups of coffee and numerous cigarettes later, Svendrup
finally nails the whole matter down. "Denmark has been a mono-
culture for about a thousand years." He pauses for emphasis and
lowers his voice. "Suddenly Danes are coming into close contact
with truly foreign peoples, and they're scared."

And that's the bottom line . . . almost. What Svendrup says
about Danes is true for Europeans in general. There is tremendous

anxiety in Europe about all things Muslim. The terrorist attacks have only exacerbated an already existing fear. Europe's headscarf headaches are not a debate about a piece of cotton cloth. They are not even about the right to religious freedom. The headscarf problem, as well as the cartoon controversy, and the advocacy of wife-beating, stoning of homosexuals, female genital mutilation, and occasional honor killings, are all focal points for the larger fear of Islamic fundamentalism and what it could do to the European identity.

Being a fundamentalist of any religion does not make you a terrorist. Fundamentalism simply means returning to the fundamentals of a religious doctrine. While some minority of extreme fundamentalists may turn to violence out of a misunderstanding of Islamic teachings, the majority of Muslim fundamentalists need not themselves be extremists. But if that is the case, why should Europe or the United States be concerned about this trend toward fundamentalism, especially among the young? The reason is that fundamentalists tend to reject many of the mainstream societal values, norms, and customs. And when they do that, they separate themselves from their society and hinder integration. Weak integration often accompanies the most intractable social ills: low and incomplete educational achievement, high unemployment and crime rates, and a strong sense of social alienation. All of these ills currently afflict too many of Europe's younger Muslims.

A handful of violent fundamentalists can threaten European and American security, but large numbers of peaceful fundamentalists threaten Europe's identity. At stake in the many values clashes is nothing less than the continent's social cohesion. If the issue is not resolved soon, it is almost certain to worsen as the influx of Muslim migrants starts to swell. Demographic forces are converging just around the corner, and when their full impact hits, they will make today's headscarf headaches seem trivial in retrospect.

Chapter 5

MIGRATION MIGRAINES

"We were asleep in the house. All of a sudden the shooting started. There was noise everywhere. We all ran for our lives. Everyone was running. I left the house and followed a group of fleeing villagers. The armed men killed everyone. They killed children and women." Roberto, who was nine years old at the time of this attack, was separated from his family, never to see them again.

Fleeing Angola with the other villagers, the young Roberto arrived in Sierra Leone, where he remained for six years until a bloody civil war forced him to flee once more. Surviving life in a Nigerian refugee camp, Roberto and 34 other Africans paid a smuggler $200 each to board a ship bound for Europe. After months in the lightless ship's hull, he was told he was on the coast of Greece. Europe at last. But the morning sun revealed street signs not in Greek, but Turkish. The ship had dropped him in Izmir, a town on the Aegean coast of Turkey. Finding his way to Istanbul and meeting up with other Africans, he kept clear of the police and sought out smugglers in Istanbul's McDonald's—the standard meeting grounds for human traffickers and their clients. Once again he engaged a smuggler to take him to Greece. In a little boat he came so close to Greece that the passengers could see the city lights. A Greek patrol boat spotted them. They were saved. Roberto and his fellow travelers waved and cheered, knowing that they would be welcomed, fed, and registered with the UN Commission on Refugees. But as the coast guard ship approached, they saw it was moving too fast. It rammed their tiny boat and let them drown. Twelve died, five survived, Roberto among them. Roberto's story, and those of many other migrants, have been chronicled in Iranian-American scholar Behzad Yaghmaian's moving book, *Embracing the Infidel.*[1] Yaghmaian reveals the traumas that many Muslims undergo before ever reaching European shores.

Just as Europe is tightening its borders and restricting its immigration and asylum laws, the number of transnational migrants is increasing. They are fleeing not only poverty, but also political repression, Islamic fundamentalism, civil wars, ethnic cleansings, and the lack of opportunity to build better lives for their children. Many do not survive the journey, falling prey to human smugglers, disease, treacherous land and sea crossings, and the despair from months or years of waiting in makeshift shelters, the holding pens for the world's estimated 19.2 million refugees.[2] Those who do survive and reach their target lands often find only new perils and frustrations as they struggle to adapt to a wholly different culture from what they left behind.

Millions of Muslims are on the move each year, most of them thrust along by globalization's invisible hand. As they enter Fortress Europe, whether by legal or illegal means, they will impact not just Europe's economic growth, but its social, political, and cultural identity as well. If their integration into European society continues along its current trajectory, only social unrest or upheaval can result. European states have belatedly awoken to this truth and are now responding with tougher immigration laws. But will they go too far?

The "Delta Plan"

In 1953, the floods for which the Dutch lowlands are famous burst their banks, leaving some 1,800 people dead in their wake. In response, the Dutch erected a series of dikes and dams to prevent a similar disaster's recurrence. The Dutch dubbed the project "The Delta Plan." After Hurricane Katrina hit the U.S. Gulf Coast on August 29, 2005, American engineers traveled to Holland to study its system of dams in preparation for the rebuilding of New Orleans. But Holland is currently erecting a new kind of Delta Plan, this time to block a flood of Muslim migrants.

As of early 2004, the population of Holland's second-largest city, Rotterdam, was half foreign. That percentage is expected to swell to 60 percent in just a decade. According to the new Delta Plan, no new refugees may settle in Rotterdam for the next five years, and no immigrants will be permitted in unless they can demonstrate an income 20 percent above the minimum wage. No new low-cost housing projects will be erected, and proficiency in the Dutch language will be a prerequisite for residency. In the wake of Van Gogh's murder, the federal government has recently turned dramatically against its once lenient immigration policies.

Rita Verdonk is Holland's tough new immigration minister. Nicknamed "Iron Rita," Verdonk has established a test for non-Western applicants seeking to immigrate to the Netherlands. One hundred thirty-eight embassies worldwide will offer the exam, which involves an initial stage of questions lasting fifteen minutes. Applicants who pass must then take two longer tests over a period of five years, and they must swear allegiance to the Dutch state. The total cost—nearly 1,500 pounds sterling, including a DVD about Holland—should place immigration out of reach for many of the world's poor. Yet the uproar over Verdonk's test has been less about the cost than about the mandatory video.

The compulsory DVD about life in Holland includes images of a topless woman bathing on the beach and two gay men kissing.

The aim is to make clear to those unfamiliar with the Netherlands that Holland is a liberal country where tolerance is a prized
value. The written exam also includes a question about the proper
response if one sees two men kissing at a nearby table in a coffee shop. Some Muslims have objected. Famile Arslan, an immigration lawyer of Turkish descent, told the *Sunday Times* that the
Dutch government was merely discriminating against non-Western immigrants under the guise of preaching toleration.[3]

The abrupt turn in Holland's approach to Muslims is striking,
and while the Van Gogh killing might seem the most obvious trig-
ger for the shift, at least one observer of Dutch politics sees deeper
roots.

"You think it's because of Van Gogh, but you can't understand
what's happening in Holland until you understand Pim Fortuijn."
Arjan Terpstra is a journalist for one of Holland's leading papers.
He has followed the country's changing political landscape closely
as both a scholar and a reporter. He tells me that the Pim phenom-
enon shook Holland's political system to its core.

The Dutch Liberal Party is identified with the color blue, while
the Labor Party is red. When these two parties, along with the
Liberal Democrats, ruled in a coalition through the early nine-
ties, they were called the purple coalition. All of their statesmen,
Terpstra says, were gray. "They were bland technocrats, discon-
nected from the problems of everyday Dutch. But there was an
undercurrent of anger and fear among ethnic Dutch who resented
what was happening in their cities," he tells me. "Fortuijn drew
on this unease with his book, *The Ruins of Eight Years of Purple*,
where he—in my opinion—skillfully overstated societal problems,
coining the phrase 'ruins,' which were never there but was eagerly
adopted by politicians on the Left and Right that saw the fall of a
powerhouse—the strong purple cabinets and national figurehead
Wim Kok." Pim was a shocking streak of color upon an otherwise
gray political canvas. And when he burst into the national spotlight, Holland could never go back to the drab old days.

Pim Fortuijn was a theatrical, in-your-face politician, who brilliantly tapped into that angry undercurrent in Dutch society, exploiting it to electrify his career. He famously declared that Holland was "full," unable to absorb any more immigrants. This notion ran counter to the prevailing liberal policy that always afforded immigrants a place of refuge, asking little of them in return.

"He understood what your average man in the street was thinking, however uninformed or ill-articulated his opinions were." Arjan has strong views on the Dutch reaction to Pim. "The butcher in the corner store, the housewife going shopping. They saw gangs of Muslim youths. There were parts of Amsterdam and other cities where the Muslims were huge, and it felt unsafe. These problems were never addressed by the gray politicians. It was taboo even to mention it.

> Immigrant issues *were* addressed before Pim Fortuijn, societal problems like Muslim youth criminality *were* studied and countered, Muslim radicalization *was* monitored, but the loud masses—who would normally hold their anti-Muslim diatribes in the privacy of their homes—chose to ignore all this and voice their uninformed opinions in the loudest way possible. The "Fortuijn revolt," as it is called now, was to a large extent a roar from the "lower belly"—a phrase that reoccurs over and over in writings on the situation. Strongly opinionated, ill-informed, emotional, irrational—imagine the scare of the sitting politicians when media forced politics to address this popular voice. They couldn't: their vocabulary didn't support it, their rationality prevented discussing things with the loud masses, who flocked to the prophet Fortuijn. In this respect, Pim was the classic demagogue.

Perhaps surprisingly, Pim's open homosexuality did not appear to hurt his popularity among this conservative segment of the populace. "I don't hate Moroccan boys," Pim once quipped. "I make love to them." Pim insisted he was not a racist; he just felt Holland should seal its borders to any further migrants.

But Pim's colorful style stirred the passions of liberals, who feared him, as well as conservatives, who praised him. His assassination in 2002 at the hands of an animal rights activist was a shocking national experience. Holland, the Dutch believed, was a peaceful, tolerant society, one welcome to all, where consensus, not violence, solved conflicts. Pim's murder marked the end of Holland's innocence.

After Pim, politicians had to tackle the immigration issue anew. The Delta Plan and subsequent demands on migrants flowed from this event. Van Gogh's slaying, a matter of true international attention, only crystallized the Islamophobia and anti-immigrant anger that Pim had raised to the surface.

"Do you think that the Dutch are just not used to dealing with foreign cultures in large numbers? I'd find that hard to believe given Holland's imperial past. It ruled much of Southeast Asia for several centuries, right?" Arjan responded:

Europe, like America, has had its share of massive people's movements, too. From the first written histories, we know there have been tribes and peoples moving back and forth over the continent, running from wars and famine or towards work and self-betterment. The Netherlands, with its history of trade—it sits at the end of three major trading rivers and borders on the North Sea, one of the busiest shipping seas—had its share of migration over the ages. We have had spasmodic growing pains, and also the gains that come from taking in immigrant groups, notably Jewish bankers and diamond workers in the seventeenth century. The big question is why we are now responding so badly to new groups.

As a country we've seen many ebbs and floods of immigration. My favorite way of expressing how idiotic the situation is now (when people like Fortuijn talk of a country that is "full") is to tell the Dutch their history. I just show them which groups came when, and then count back to 2,500 years ago, when there were exactly zero original ethnic Dutchmen around. Every group has hence migrated into our little swamp at one point. We're an immigrant country if ever there was one.

"One positive point," Arjan notes, is that funding for integration programs has become much easier to get. "With the scare of social upheaval in their minds, government officials are now lavish in funding anything that can help build, or rebuild, social cohesion into the fabric of society. Friends of mine work in societal organizations, and get every government grant they request, as long as it supports the words 'social cohesion' somewhere on the title page. Five years ago this was definitely not the case."

Let's Do the Numbers

It's New Year's Eve 2020 and you have been invited to a very unusual party. You find yourself in a room with 99 other people, all of whom have come to celebrate the world's great diversity. To underscore the party's theme, all one hundred guests exactly mirror, on a very tiny scale, the proportional ethnic composition of the world's 7.8 billion people. Scanning the room and doing some quick arithmetic, you notice that 56 guests come from Asia: 19 Chinese and 17 Indians. Sixteen come from Africa, 13 of those from the sub-Saharan region. Seven of your evening companions hail from Eastern Europe and the former Soviet Union, while 5 are from Western Europe. Only 4 call the United States their home, and only 3 were born in the Middle East.

Your hosts have planned their party with even greater care. They have also made their invitees reflect the world's other seismic demographic shifts. The majority of guests live in cities, reflecting the first time in history that most of the world's inhabitants no longer toil in the countryside. And the party planners have projected out to 2050, making 16 guests aged 65 or older. The hosts know that by that year the elderly population will have tripled to 1.5 billion. Many of the elderly will contrast sharply with the guests representing the counter-trend—the globe's next big baby boom, found predominantly in Muslim states: Pakistan, Afghanistan, Saudi Arabia, Yemen, and Iraq. If you arrive late to the party and peer around the room, you may be struck by an age and color correlation: the white Christian Europeans will be older, while the Asian Muslims will be young, restive, and mobile.

As the evening wanes, you find yourself engaged in more serious conversations with the other guests, and the talk turns philosophical. Soon you discover something unexpected. Many of those from Africa and Latin America are Christians. Your notion of a typical white Christian is being challenged because Europe is no longer the world's center of Christianity. Overhearing some other discussions around the room, you notice an undercurrent of tension rippling through the crowds. Christians and Muslims from Asia, Africa, and Latin America are preaching the virtues of their religions, hoping to convert the non-believing guests. Suddenly the New Year's cheer has vanished from the room, and you sense that the celebration of diversity has only exposed the cleavages between cultures, age cohorts, and religions.

Demographers are keenly aware of a looming crisis in aging which lurks just around the corner, but policymakers have been slow to take precautionary measures. The number of elderly is rising sharply as life expectancy increases in the industrialized nations. The world's median age today is roughly 24, but by 2050 it is projected to be 44, and 53 to 55 in Germany and Japan. Western Europe and Japan will gray the most. Italy, for example, is on track to have more than 1 million people over the age of 90 by 2025.[4] At the same time that Europe's mortality rate is falling, so too is its birthrate. Ethnic Europeans are having fewer children, and consequently their populations are shrinking. And with them shrinks the labor force. By 2050, Japan is expected to see its workforce—those aged between 16 and 64—drop by an extraordinary 37 percent. Italy's workforce will fall by an even greater 39 percent, and Germany's by 18 percent. France and Great Britain will experience declines of 11 and 12 percent. Conversely, the United States' workforce is expected to grow by 33 percent.[5]

What happens to societies with aging populations and shrinking numbers of workers? Someone has to support those who retire. In most industrialized countries today, the ratio of workers to pensioners is 4:1, but by 2050 that ratio may drop to just 2:1. A halving of workers to retirees will put enormous strains on societies with aging populations, and Europe will likely face some critical readjustments as a result. Policymakers could attempt to lessen the crisis by encouraging delayed retirements. Maintaining a graying workforce could increase productivity, but this would require a major shift in long-held social values which place a high premium on the ability to retire in one's sixties. But even such a change may not suffice to support the elderly who cannot work. If Europeans hope to maintain their living standards in retirement, more young workers will have to be found. A logical place to look will be to those regions currently experiencing baby booms, namely, parts of the Muslim world.

How Did We Get Here?

Although Muslims have lived in Europe for many centuries, the major wave of Muslim immigration in the modern era began following the First World War and continued through the period of decolonization. Britain and France began absorbing Muslims from South Asia and the Maghreb respectively to help with reconstruction following both world wars. To help rebuild its own shattered postwar economy, Germany invited many Muslim guest workers from Turkey, expecting that these guests would one day return home. But finding conditions more agreeable in their new surroundings, many remained, sent for wives, and began families. As the author Max Frisch put it: "Wir riefen Arbeiter, aber Menschen kamen." ("We called for workers, but people came.") A similar pattern developed in the other major European states, although

Britain, France, and Holland tended naturally to attract Muslims from their former colonies.

During Germany's postwar reconstruction and ensuing economic miracle, Turkey, Morocco, and Tunisia were eager to sign agreements with Germany encouraging their citizens to migrate as guest workers. Because the Muslim countries faced difficult economic times, the guest-worker program offered a chance to reduce the number of unemployed young men at home while simultaneously increasing their foreign exchange reserves coming in the form of remittances these workers sent to their families back home. Today and for the foreseeable future, as Muslim states in North Africa and the Middle East, as well as those in South Asia and Indonesia, have growing young populations but struggling economies, these states and their citizens will aggressively seek labor opportunities. Just as in the past, Europe will be an attractive target.

Although immigrants currently represent only 2 percent of world population, they represent a critical revenue stream for their countries of origin. Even at today's relatively low 2 percent level, immigrants have a far greater impact than their numbers might suggest. They send home nearly $67 billion per year, and in many cases, such as for Mexico, their remittances constitute their home country's primary income stream.

Immigrants are also expanding their range of target countries. Beyond the United States, Canada, Australia, and New Zealand, migrants from poorer nations are traveling to Greece, Italy, Hungary, and the Czech Republic, as well as to oil-rich nations in the Middle East. Most transnational migratory laborers are rural people, but they often settle in cities, making their transition that much harder. When migrants transplant themselves in sufficient numbers, they typically change their host country's character.

None of this necessarily means that European states will encourage Muslim immigration to solve their labor shortage, but it does mean that migratory labor from the developing world, and particularly the Muslim world, will be drawn to Europe, not least because large Muslim communities are already in place in several other West European countries. If the European states choose to draw more heavily on this labor pool, they will need to make citizens out of them. And as more and more Muslims are enfranchised, their political power will continue to grow.

Each year, Europe receives approximately half a million new immigrants and 400,000 asylum seekers, many of whom are Muslims. There is also an annual estimated influx of between 120,000 to 500,000 illegal immigrants.[6] EU Justice and Home Affairs Commissioner António Vitorino has made plain that Europe must attract immigrants to satisfy its labor shortage, but he admits that Muslims have been difficult to integrate. In an interview with the German newspaper *Die Zeit*, Commissioner Vitorino was asked how Muslim immigrants should be expected to behave. He responded that all immigrants, regardless of their country of origin, must learn their host country's language, respect democracy and the secular state, and preserve equal rights for both sexes. But he added that immigrants from Muslim states have tended to isolate themselves, making their integration more difficult. "Fundamentalism," Vitorino insisted, "cannot be accepted."[7]

The Age of Migration

For ethnic Europeans, globalization is knitting together Europe's economies and politics, in turn creating a European identity. For Europe's Muslims, however, aspects of globalization, from the spread of Muslim global media to the rise in Muslim migration, are producing the opposite result. Rather than uniting, globalization is dividing. It is too often encouraging a religious over a secular identity and forging dangerous fault lines in Europe's fragile experiment.

One of the most difficult problems wrought by globalization continues to be the massive and rapid transplantation of foreign cultures into the Old World. Waves of immigrants have been washing upon Europe's shores since World War II, but those waves are likely to rise. The world is entering what Prof. Stephen Castles has dubbed "the age of migration," a century in which demographic trends have the potential to destabilize previously peaceful societies and critically reconfigure formerly homogenous states. Castles, one of the leading scholars of international migration, predicts that this century will witness the greatest transfer of human capital in history. Widening gaps between rich and poor nations, increasing numbers of free-trade agreements, and proliferating wars will all, he believes, send unprecedented numbers of migrants on the march. Add to this Europe's aging population and attendant labor shortage, and the youth bulge in Muslim states, and the likely result will be that many more young Muslims will be drawn to Europe, just as they were in the postwar decades. Demographic growth, Castles notes, has usually accompanied political conflict and war, and although international migration has long been a salient feature of human history, it has never been as pervasive or as socioeconomically significant as it is today.[8]

Across new immigration lands, especially in Europe, we are witnessing challenges to national identity as migrants and their offspring rise in number. As Castles puts it: "The nation-state, as it has developed since the eighteenth century, is premised on the idea of cultural as well as political unity. This unity has often been fictitious—a construct of the ruling elite—but it has provided powerful national myths."[9] Castles' point is that sudden, large numbers of immigrants are bound to reshape, or at the very least threaten, the host country's historic identity.

Europe is not alone in its struggle to integrate migrants. Demographers estimate that Japan, the fastest shrinking and aging nation on earth, will have only half its current population of 120 million by the century's end. Within just thirty years, Japan will already have 30 percent fewer inhabitants and 1 million 100-year-olds. Like Europe, Japan cannot sustain its current living standard without importing immigrant labor. And like Europe, Japan's largely homogenous society finds it difficult to accept foreigners on equal terms.

Akio and Yoshi Nakashima are mid-thirties, hard-working, tax-paying parents of two children. They live in an orderly suburban home in Tokyo, and like most parents they worry about their children's futures. But the Nakashimas worry about their children's chances to find good jobs for only one reason—they are not Japanese. Though both parents and children possess fluent Japanese, Akio and Yoshi are Vietnamese, former boat people who arrived twenty-one years ago. To this day the parents have no Japanese friends. Socially speaking, their integration has been muted at best.[10]

The United Nations estimates that Japan will need 17 million immigrants by 2050 to sustain its living standards, pension system, and keep the economy afloat. That figure would represent 18 percent of the population, while immigrants currently comprise only 1 percent of the population. Such a dramatic influx of foreigners could turn Japan upside-down and inside-out with the ensuing social change. Of course, Japan may be able to fill some of its economic needs by incorporating its women more fully into the labor force. Either way, the coming decades portend significant changes for Japan as well as Europe. How each absorbs its immigrants will play a major part in their economic and political future on the international stage.

Baby Boom, or Just a Whimper?

Even without an influx of new immigrants, Europe's Muslim populations are rising in number. Estimates vary widely, but the U.S. State Department's annual World Survey on Religious Freedom for 2003 conservatively assumes that there are 23 million Muslims in Europe, 5 percent of the population. This figure does not include Turkey, which, if incorporated into the EU, would elevate that number to 90 million, or 15 percent. The Muslim birthrate is triple that of ethnic Europeans, and the percentages of young

Muslims across the continent already surpass their ethnic European age cohorts. The total Muslim population is expected to double by 2015, while the ethnic European population is likely to decline by 3.5 percent.

Within the largest European states themselves, these demographic shifts will be even more pronounced. Prof. Philip Martin has observed that the ethnic German population is projected to decline to 62 million by the year 2030, making foreigners 17 percent of the total population. In this scenario, the population of major cities such as Frankfurt and Stuttgart would be half foreign within two generations. Other projections of even higher fertility rates among immigrants suggest that Germany will be 30 percent foreign by 2030.[11] Many of these will be Muslims. Some estimates project France's Muslim population to reach one-fourth by 2025. In Holland, major cities such as Rotterdam could be majority non-ethnic Dutch within a decade. Much of this extraordinary growth is a result of the high Muslim birthrates and the existence of sizeable Muslim youth bulges.

Philip Longman, who has studied the global "birth dearth" extensively, concludes that the future belongs to what he calls "the fundamentalist moment." Longman maintains that only fundamentalists, who believe they are commanded by God to produce many children, will account for any rises within populations.[12] If Longman is correct, then Muslims in Europe and the United States will see their ranks swell as those of other religions decline. As Mustafa Yoldaş told me, if the ethnic Europeans would just have more children, they wouldn't be as nervous about Muslims. "We [Muslims] believe in having kids," he said.

Despite the impressive sounding numbers, demographic projections must always be taken with a large grain of salt. Speculations about the future are invariably based on extrapolations of current trends, and trends can change. The U.S. Census Bureau, for example, had to revise its predictions for South Africa. In 2000 it projected that country's population to rise by 6 million people in

2025. As a result of the unexpectedly rampant spread of AIDS, the Bureau now expects South Africa's population to fall by 9 million by that year. Aside from unexpected outbreaks and natural disasters, there are other reasons to question the explosive nature of Muslim birthrates. As minorities in a society enter into the middle class, they often adopt the reproductive patterns of the majority. If Europe's Muslims improve their social and economic standing, it is possible that they will tend toward having fewer children than at present. We are now witnessing the births of the fourth generation of post–World War II children of Muslim immigrants, and so far birthrates remain high. However, Muslims on the whole still represent part of the underclass, overrepresented in unemployment, lower wage earnings, and political disenfranchisement. In short, many of Europe's Muslims are struggling second-class citizens, if they are citizens at all. If more of them are brought into the middle class, their reproductive patterns might start to resemble other, less fertile, ethnic groups.

Power Shifts

Demographic shifts and migratory patterns are two ineluctable pressures upon Europe in the twenty-first century. But yet another trend threatens Europe's identity: the world's rising need for energy. As China and India continue to modernize at a dizzying pace, followed by other smaller but still burgeoning economies in Southeast Asia and beyond, their increasing levels of energy consumption will drive world market prices ever higher. Greater energy expenditures will reduce Europe's available resources for other needs. Those cuts will most likely hit social services. Thus, the poorest in society, which typically includes recent immigrants, and which currently means the Muslim underclass, will suffer the most, a scenario certain only to exacerbate Europe's integration dilemma.

Cassandras have long predicted the end of world oil resources, yet exploration has always unearthed previously undiscovered supplies. Today, however, the situation may at last be changing. We may have reached the point where technology is sufficiently sophisticated that all of the earth's major oil fields have now been located. New sources may be found, but their yields are not expected to alter the overall downward trend.

Assessing the debate among energy experts, Jeremy Rifkin, head of a Washington-based think tank on global trends and consultant to the German government, argues persuasively that even under the most optimistic scenarios, world oil supplies will peak within the next twenty to thirty years. Although oil supplies will remain to be exploited, Rifkin believes that the simple law of supply and demand will drive prices significantly higher. Once it is clear that the supply peak has been reached and humanity begins struggling over ever diminishing supplies, world oil prices will invariably rise. At that point a new influx of wealth will flow into that country which sits atop the greatest supply.[13]

Saudi Arabia's power in international affairs, Rifkin maintains, will reach new heights unmatched by the 1970s, when it wielded the oil embargo against America with devastating effectiveness. Flush with even greater wealth, how will the Saudi kingdom spend its riches? Most likely it will continue to do what it has been doing for decades, namely, export its fundamentalist brand of Islam to the Muslim diaspora, only more so. Europe's Muslims, already beneficiaries of mosques and educational programs compliments of Saudi largesse, will probably become recipients of even greater amounts of Saudi petro dollars. These funds will be invested in the construction of more mosques, more training in Wahabism, and the closening of ties between Europe's Muslims and Saudi imams. In short, the coming rise in world oil prices could translate into greater Saudi influence among Europe's Muslim millions. If, when that day arrives, Europe's Muslims are still poorly integrated into European society—underprivileged, alienated, and angry—their susceptibility to extremist messages may prove explosive.

Dismal Indications

On the first anniversary of 9/11, a group of Muslim extremists gathered at the Finsbury Park mosque and declared that the attacks on America were justified. They called Osama bin Laden a hero. One imam remarked that only believers see Bin Laden as a hero and only hypocrites hate him. Under the leadership of Abu-Hamza al-Masri, the Supporters of Sharia operated out of the Finsbury Park mosque and sought a return to a pure Islamic state. Although al-Masri is at last in jail and the Finsbury mosque has been purged of its radical elements, the kind of radical sentiments he espoused remain.

Across major British cities, extremist voices are easily accessible to the young. Saudi pamphlets are readily available in large cities such as Birmingham, inviting young Muslim men, many of whom are unemployed, to study the Quran in Medina for three years. In recent years many mosques have switched from preaching in Urdu or Arabic to English, as a means of reaching out to younger generations, and some of the more radical mosques have found this useful in recruiting the young. Since the London underground attacks, of course, all such mosques have come under even greater scrutiny. But scrutinizing sermons is only half the battle. The other half involves reducing the likelihood that young people will be receptive to extreme ideas. Part of that problem requires redressing social imbalances, and current indicators do not look good.

Whenever youth unemployment is exceptionally high, you have a recipe for trouble. Pakistanis and Bangladeshis, who comprise the bulk of Britain's Muslims, tend to be overrepresented in unemployment and underemployment. Twice as many of these Muslims work in manual as opposed to white-collar labor, compared to non-Muslim whites. They earn on average two-thirds that of their non-Muslim white counterparts, and when self-employed, they earn only three-fourths the income of non-Muslim whites.[14]

Their illiteracy rate is higher than other ethnic groups, and although they represent between 2.9 and 3.6 percent of the population, Muslims constitute a disproportionate percent of prison inmates. While crime among Muslims may be high, tensions are exacerbated by the lack of Muslims within the police force.

These trends persist when comparing Muslim Europeans to other European immigrant groups. British Muslims of Pakistani origin are three times as likely to be jobless as British Hindus. More surprising still, Indian Muslims in Britain are twice as likely to be unemployed as Indian Hindus. Pakistanis and Bangladeshis have an unemployment rate 2.5 times that of whites, and they are three times as likely to be in low-paid jobs. British Muslims are greatly overrepresented in poverty, many living in overcrowded, subsidized homes.

And the trends are not encouraging. National studies of students' performance in recent years show significant improvement for many ethnic minorities. Black and Caribbean pupils are on an upward trend, Chinese and other Asians are more often receiving top grades, and students of Indian origin are proving the highest academic achievers. But for young Muslims the story is the reverse. Pakistani children's gains are below that of their ethnic peers, and Bangladeshi pupils are actually declining in their school performance.[15]

Britain is unique among European states in that most of its Muslims are citizens and enjoy the right to vote. They exercise that right more fully than their white compatriots. They participate actively in local politics, typically voting for Labour candidates, which is why the Respect Party victory in Bethnal Green was so significant. Among the younger generations, surveys find that most in this voting population identify themselves first as Muslims, second as members of a particular ethnic or racial group. If they continue to vote along religious lines, in other words if a genuine "Muslim voting bloc" emerges, resentment at their social standing will surely be felt at the ballot box.

Affirmative Action, French Style

The riots that racked France in November 2005 began in the mainly Muslim suburbs of Paris. Vastly overrepresented in poverty, crime, and unemployment (Muslim men's unemployment rate is twice the national average), Muslims have been poorly integrated into French society. Predominantly segregated in communities around major cities such as Paris (where 38 percent of France's Muslims live) and Marseilles (which is one-quarter Muslim), these Muslims exist in ghettos of depressed neighborhoods, reinforcing their alienation from the larger society. In order to redress some of these economic disparities, the French government has engaged in a type of affirmative action since 1998, giving Muslim citizens, particularly the young, greater employment opportunities in the public sector.[16] Despite proactive measures by the state, progress for French Muslims has been limited. Following the riots, the French government pledged anew to redress the economic inequities plaguing the Muslim population.

Algeria is the country of origin for the largest number—1.5 million—of France's Muslims, while some 350,000 Tunisians form the next largest group. But France is also home to the same number of asylum seekers. And not all of France's Muslims are Arabs, for some 315,000 Turks also reside there. Nearly half of the country's Muslims are citizens, which has implications for the formation of political pressure groups. More than 1,000 Islamic associations and ten Muslim cultural associations exist across France, as well as many ethnic organizations, which include mostly Muslims. Although many of these groups focus on charitable or educational issues, there are also fundamentalist and Islamist groups who profit from the freedoms of a democratic state. Funded by the World Islamic League in Saudi Arabia, the Tabligh movement, like the Turkish Milli Görüş, seeks a return to traditional Islamic ways, stricter observance of Islamic laws and customs, and an end to corrupt governments. Some scholars believe that the rising pan-

Islamic sentiment will not hinder Muslim integration into Europe, but will aid it by providing a group identity and enabling constructive associations for the peaceful resolution of social inequities. In that respect, Islamic organizations could serve as an alternative to extremism, unless, of course, some of those organizations are themselves extremist.[17]

Homogenous No More

Germany, even more than France or Britain, has endured the growing pains of ethnic and cultural change. For decades German statesmen could believe that Germany was not a land of immigrants. But according to the Independent Commission on Migration's thorough 2001 report, "The political and normative guiding principle of the past that 'Germany is not a country of immigrants' has become untenable as the maxim of migration and integration policy. More and more people are becoming aware that migration to Germany involves both enrichment and problems."[18] With a total foreign population of roughly 7.3 million, or 8.9 percent of the populace, the demographic trends on foreigners alone do not bode well for a country with weak integration, let alone one anxious about "foreign" peoples. According to a 2005 survey, only 34 percent of Germans view immigration from the Middle East and North Africa as a good thing, while 57 percent view it negatively.[19] The figures are roughly the same concerning immigrants from Eastern Europe, but Muslim immigrants bear the added burden of rising Islamophobia.

Turks constitute three-quarters of Germany's entire Muslim population, and studies of the third generation find them less integrated than their parents or grandparents. Their knowledge of German is weak, their high school dropout rate is high, and this has resulted in considerably higher unemployment rates, crime rates, and social alienation.[20] Mosques have stepped in to fill the gap, providing Quranic education and a sense of community, but in turn the young become even less connected to their larger society. Such a situation, if left unchecked, could leave young Muslims susceptible to radical messages.

The problem begins at an early age. Since most Turks in Germany hail from the poorer, less literate regions of eastern Anatolia and, like most immigrants, tend to settle within geographically close communities, the children are raised in homes where distinctive dialects are spoken, parents are unable to read to their children in German, and less contact with ethnic Germans is available. One Berlin daycare worker with 22 years' experience described the situation as rapidly deteriorating. Her preschool class is representative of this trend. Of her 15 students, 13 are Turks, one is Polish, and one is ethnically German. Consequently, the Turkish children speak mainly among themselves, and they enter the school system with insufficient language skills. For Muslim girls, the situation worsens as they enter middle and high school, as their parents forbid them to attend school trips, participate in mixed-gender sports, dance at clubs with their classmates, or go swimming with their peers. Such parentally enforced separation presents serious barriers to integration.

Social standing has not substantially improved for teenage and young Turkish Germans, despite being third-generation residents. Roughly one-quarter of all Turkish Germans are under age 30, and they are still perceived as "guests" by many ethnic Germans, even though they have lived in Germany all their lives and some speak better German than Turkish. Approximately 17 percent complete the Abitur exams, and only 40 percent obtain vocational training. When questioned about their views on religious matters, a surprising trend appeared. Forty-one percent of 18- to 25-year-olds agreed that charging interest is against their religion, compared to 26- to 29 year-olds, of whom only 38 percent agreed, and those 30 and older, of whom 34 percent agreed.[21]

In response to some of these challenges, Berlin and other German cities have created more specialized adult literacy programs for foreign-born workers. When it was discovered that Muslim mothers were only willing to attend such programs if their young children were with them rather than left in daycare centers, the literacy programs were adapted and experienced much greater success. Unfortunately, federal and state funding to such programs has been cut in recent years as the German economy continues to stagnate.

Releasing the Pressure Valve

In the face of daunting demographic pressures, from high Muslim birthrates and global immigration patterns, combined with the looming threat of shifting power balances and rising energy costs, how can Europe solve its Muslim dilemma? Oxford historian Timothy Garton Ash believes that Europe can learn much from America. Calling for a European version of "Californication," Garton Ash thinks the answer lies in intermarriage between ethnic Europeans and Muslim residents, as assimilation of the latter into the larger society will naturally follow. Here is how he puts it, "Look at the demographic map of the world, and you will see one continent above all that needs either a massive baby boom or large-scale immigration to sustain its ageing population. That continent is Europe. Much of our immigration is likely to come from the Muslim world. In theory, it should be easier for Turks, Moroccans, Algerians and Pakistanis to feel at home in Europe than in America, because Europe is just a loose, diverse continent rather than a single nation. In practice, it's the other way round. So we should learn from the Americans. What Europe needs is more Californication."[22]

Garton Ash is correct that California has, in part, achieved some degree of racial mixing and subsequent assimilation of diverse ethnic groups, but in America overall less than 2 percent of marriages are interracial, and Hurricane Katrina exposed how much racial tension remains in America. Europe may be even more resistant to such a solution. Though Californication may have its undeniable merits, there are other options open to Europe as it struggles with integration issues.

As Muslim minorities wax in number and gain a louder political voice, their opinions over European and American activities in the Muslim world will grow in significance. Today, many of Europe's Muslims do not yet enjoy the full rights of citizenship, particularly the right of suffrage. Without the right to vote, these minorities have no peaceful political outlet for redressing their grievances. Their objection to second-class status is therefore increasingly likely to assume a hostile character. But given the right to vote, their influence could come to alter the trajectory of European foreign policies, particularly regarding issues ranging from the Middle East to relations with America. Their impact on European domestic policies, however, will likely be far greater.

Muslim ambivalence toward mainstream American and European values manifests itself in ways beyond political protest or rising religiosity. Purchasing patterns also reflect identity politics. One hint of what may be to come can be seen in the present trend toward Islamically-inspired products and services. For some, these products reflect religious values that Muslims feel are superior to mainstream European or American norms. For others, buying these consumer goods is their own way of waging economic jihad.

Chapter 6

CLASH OF THE BARBIES

Razanne is a demure, dark-skinned Muslim girl. She wears the hijab and dutifully prays five times daily. Standing 11″ high, she cuts an unlikely figure as a frontline soldier in Muslim Europe's economic jihad. But as her American creators stress, it is not how one looks that matters, but what one's heart and acts reveal.

It may not seem as epic a struggle as Samuel Huntington's *Clash of Civilizations*, but on a doll-sized scale the battle is just as fierce. For more than four decades the Mattel toy company has dominated the doll market with Barbie, the buxom, chic, glamour girl who has delighted little girls around the world since her introduction in 1959. According to some estimates, a Barbie doll is sold every two seconds somewhere on the globe. Barbie has penetrated 150 countries, netting annual revenues of over $1 billion. With an array of ethnic and multicultural spin-offs (Japanese, Indian, African-American), Barbies have touched the lives of girls from nearly all walks of life—with one notable exception. The one group not wholly beguiled by her charms has been the Muslim market.

Mattel's Muslim Barbie never quite caught on. Leila, a doll in sultry garb, was based on an eighteenth-century tale of a sultan's concubine, not exactly the role model which Muslim parents wished to give their daughters. Leila and all Barbies are banned in Saudi Arabia on grounds that they promote vice through their immodest clothes. Toy-sellers in Saudi Arabia are fined and the dolls confiscated if they are discovered in shops.[1] Instead, Syrian-based Fulla, introduced in November 2003, is promoted there and throughout the Middle East, along with a whole line of accoutrements and related products.

Iran also opposes Barbie. Sara and Dara are the Iranian toy challengers, each intended as 8-year-olds. One of the problems with Barbie, according to the Iranian Institute for the Intellectual Development of Children and Young Adults, is Ken. It is inappropriate for a young girl or woman to have a boyfriend. Barbie's "wanton" lifestyle and materialism directly contradict Iranian Muslim values.[2]

Many Muslim parents in Europe, America, and the Muslim diaspora share, to some extent, the official Saudi and Iranian objection to Barbie's immodesty. And according to Noor Saadeh, who with her husband created Razanne, a surprising number of non-Muslim parents have also expressed support for their creation. "We're not criticizing America or anyone," Noor says. "We just want to give our daughters an alternative doll to play with."

Appleton, Wisconsin, might seem an unlikely birthplace for the founder of a Muslim Barbie, but that is indeed where Noor Saadeh grew up. Noor was raised in a Christian home, attending church regularly, like most everyone else in town. As a young woman she moved to New York in order to pursue a career as an opera singer. Egyptians she met there introduced her to Islam, and as she read the Quran and learned more about the religion, Noor found that "things just began to click." She tells me, "The Quran is an amazing book of psychology. It really explains how people are and why they act the way they do."

When Noor later returned to Appleton, she discovered that a Muslim community and a small mosque had sprung up. She soon began teaching children in that mosque, and then she had an idea.

"We took some of the popular songs kids like, and we Islamicized the lyrics. We put it on a cassette, and it just took off." According to Noor, her music has now been illegally pirated around the Muslim world, and she couldn't be happier about it. Four years after converting, Noor married Ammar, a Palestinian, and the two settled in Dallas, where they run their doll-making business and raise their son.

"How did you first get the idea for Razanne?" I ask.

"My husband and I started making her in 1999, but I had been thinking about it before then. It was around Eid time that I saw all the little girls in the community getting Barbies as gifts, and I wished we could give something comparable to Muslim girls, but a doll not as womanly as Barbie. I felt certain that there must be other parents who were thinking the same thing."

If Barbie were 5'6" instead of 11½" tall, her measurements would be 39-21-33. It is rumored that an academic once calculated the probability of a woman's being shaped like Barbie at less than 1 in 100,000.[3] Razanne is a more modestly figured doll with a pre-teen's body. "We know that girls do a lot of psychological modeling. They imitate and act out what they observe in the role models given to them. We want girls to know that their character is more important than the way they look." "You know, Zach," Noor adds, "women are constantly judged by their faces or their bodies. When we, as Muslim women, cover ourselves, it makes a statement that we will have to be taken seriously for who we are on the inside." Noor, herself, wears a headscarf, but not a veil, and she dresses in long, unrevealing attire. "My friends joked with me after we produced the first Razanne. They all said, 'Noor, she looks just like you!'"

"How did your parents feel about your conversion to Islam?"

"Actually, they were okay with it. The thing they really had trouble with was my covering myself. When religion is something inside you, it doesn't bother anyone, but when it affects your outer appearance, then it somehow seems harder to face. Eventually, my mom came around, and now she is even proud of the fact that I cover. She's been great."

"You grew up in Appleton, and now you and your husband live in Dallas. I've been to Dallas, and I have friends who were raised in Appleton. These are not places I imagine having large Muslim communities. What's it like for you there?"

"Well, I was amazed to find a community in Appleton. It definitely did not exist when I was a child. And you'd be very surprised by Dallas. It's extremely cosmopolitan. Every day I see women in headscarves all around town. We live not far from the downtown mosque.[4] And folks come up to me all the time to ask me about Islam. They say things like, 'You don't even have an accent. Where are you from?' They're always polite and curious. I've never had anyone mistreat me here. I always try to answer their questions. I want people to understand that Muslim women live normal lives: we have jobs, we volunteer, and we have fun, too."

To make clear that Razanne is a modern Muslim woman, the Saadehs have created several versions of the doll. Praying Razanne wears a long, pastel-colored gown and is accompanied by a prayer rug. There is also a Teacher Razanne, dressed in a two-piece business suit with briefcase and mini-laptop; a Muslim Scout Razanne, who comes with a CD of Islamic summer-camp cheers sung by children; an Eid Mubarak Razanne, dressed in her best clothes with accessories to help her celebrate the holiday; and an In and Out Razanne, showing the doll at home, dressed in typical Western clothes with an additional, covering outfit for going out. This last Razanne stresses that Muslim women have fun, but they dress appropriately for different contexts. "We're trying to break down stereotypes—one doll at a time." A Doctor Razanne is on the way, as is Community Service Razanne, who donates her time at the local hospital. The dolls come in your choice of three skin tones: Caucasian, East Indian, and African.

Razanne is slowly penetrating European markets as well as toy markets in some Muslim states. The Saadehs have launched distributorships in Britain, Germany, Malaysia, and the Middle East, as well as in Hong Kong, where the doll is manufactured. But for now the 30,000 units sold annually are unlikely to catch even Barbie's eye. More than 1 billion Barbies have been sold since 1959, making her one of the best-selling dolls in history. Annual sales typically exceed $1 billion. Barbie is an economic powerhouse that Razanne could not hope to topple, but it is not on the economic front that Razanne poses her true challenge.

The rise of Muslim businesses represents something deeper than just a capitalist enterprise filling a niche market. It is a direct response to perceived American values. Islamically based businesses aim to make profits, like any other enterprise. What they do not want is to advance un-Islamic values. Through their products and their corporate practices, many of these emerging Muslim companies promote values such as charity, modesty, respect for workers, community service, poverty reduction, and more. They pose a moral, not just an economic, challenge to the American consumer culture. They are seizing the presumed moral high ground, using the values question as their key selling point.

In a way, the growth of Islamic enterprises can be viewed as one act in the drama of "Jihad vs. McWorld," as Benjamin Barber predicted more than a decade ago, though it is not unfolding exactly as he foresaw. Barber described a global battle between two foes. On one side stood McWorld, the goliath force of wild capitalism, relentlessly invading all corners of the globe, converting the conquered to wanton consumerism. On the other side, dwarfed in size but not in fervor, stood Jihad: average citizens fighting a furious rearguard action in defense of traditional cultures, "family values," and local norms. The patterns Barber recognized ten years ago are even more pronounced today, but with one notable exception. Rather than protecting local traditions and customs through anti-capitalist means, Muslim enterprises are boldly attacking McWorld on its home turf—in the marketplace. They are fighting fire with fire, doll with doll.

When I shared this idea with Noor, she objected to the battle metaphor. She fears that the typical consumer will think that Muslims want to take over their McWorld, which is not the case. She offered an example of how McWorld seems to be encroaching on her own world.

"A few years ago my husband, son and I made the small hajj to Mecca. For any Muslim this is a lifelong dream, even just making the smaller pilgrimage. It was our first glimpse of the Kaaba—this simple but beloved edifice to which all Muslims turn when they pray. Seeing the constant circumambulation of the Kaaba and actually joining the throng gives you the feeling that this is the center of the universe and all of life sort of boils down to this undulating, revolving circle that goes around it 24/7, stopping only for the five prayers each day."

"Upon exiting our first day I saw, much to my sadness and frustration, the Golden Arches directly across the street, along with a number of other Western fast-food restaurants. Granted there are an awful lot of people to feed there, especially during hajj season, but my disappointment that the Saudis had plopped a McDonald's restaurant in a place that most people visit to forget the world and concentrate just on worship for a few days was actually overwhelming. Here? Right in front of the Kaaba? Not out of sight on a side street at least? To me it was if Western consumerism was saying 'We're here! Right at the doorstep of your most sacred site in Islam!' Who wants to take over whom, I ask you?"

Whether Razanne bests Barbie on the economic battlefront is not at issue. She need only survive and flourish to remain a threat to McWorld. The true battleground on which Razanne's mettle, and that of other Islamic businesses—enterprises specifically designed to promote Muslim values and further Muslim causes—will be tested is not in the traditional Muslim world, where states can tip the balance in her favor, but in Europe, where a burgeoning Muslim counterculture grows stronger by the day.

Brand America

From 1980 to 2000, global trade nearly tripled, and much of that growth resulted not solely from aggressive American corporate strategies and the opening of new markets with the end of the Cold War, but also from the popularity of American brand names. By 2000, sixty-two of the most popular one hundred brand names belonged to U.S. firms. But in 2000, as resentment of American global dominance spiked, the long trend began to show real signs of reversing. Local brands revived in popularity as consumers preferred to patronize smaller firms using local materials and labor.

According to a 2004 report by the New York consulting firm NOP World (which merged with GfK Aktiengesellschaft in 2005 to form GfK NOP), American brand names are losing ground to non-American competitors. The study's authors conducted in-depth interviews with some 30,000 consumers in more than thirty countries. The results were unmistakable. Being too closely associated with the United States is a turnoff to many consumers around the world. NOP World's then managing director, Tom Miller (now with Ipsos), noted that even though the overall economic losses might not yet be severe, losing even 1 percent of sales can have a significant impact on a company. Miller believes that, "We're seeing a shift in the balance of brand-power."

Noreena Hertz is one of Britain's "whiz kids." Having earned a college degree at age 19 and a Wharton MBA at 23, she went on to advise the Russian government on privatization issues. Now she serves as the associate director of the Centre for International Business and Management at Cambridge University. After extensively researching global consumer purchasing patterns, she found that 20 percent of consumers in Britain refused to buy certain products on ethical grounds, and a further 29 percent did not buy products because of environmental concerns. According to her studies, the brand power of several major U.S. firms, such as Microsoft, McDonald's, Nike, Disney, and the Discovery Channel, has been hard hit in recent years. Meanwhile, foreign firms such as Philips, Sony, BMW, and Volkswagen have all gained on their American competitors. Trust in three major U.S. brand names—Yahoo, MTV, and Citibank—has plummeted. Another study by the Edelman Public Relations firm found that 66 percent of Americans trusted the Coca-Cola brand, while only 40 percent of Europeans do.[5] The same survey revealed that 66 percent of Germans and 64 percent of French said they were less inclined to buy American products because of U.S. foreign policy.

Adding his voice to the growing concern is Prof. John Quelch, senior associate dean for international development at Harvard's Business School. Quelch has cautioned that the anti-Americanism which major U.S. corporations are now experiencing is not simply a blip on the otherwise steady EKG of global consumer patterns. Quelch perceives a longer-term trend. "Never before have global concerns about American foreign policy so threatened to change consumer behavior. . . . We are not speaking here of the frivolous grandstanding associated with temporary boycotts by a student minority. We are witnessing the emergence of a consumer lifestyle with broad international appeal that is grounded in a rejection of American capitalism, American foreign policy, and Brand America."[6]

Quelch's subsequent research suggested that his earlier assertions may have been overstated, particularly regarding Muslims. He later found that while anti-globalization buying patterns account for 13 percent of world consumers, Muslim shoppers are no more opposed to American brands than are non-Muslims. Quelch surveyed consumers in Egypt, Turkey, and Indonesia, and compared their responses to those in the United Kingdom, Japan, France, Poland, South Africa, Brazil, China, and India. Examining the top half of income earners in those countries, Quelch asked respondents how they felt about major American brands: Nike, Ford, Motorola, Kraft, Exxon-Mobil, as well as Coke and Pepsi. According to Quelch and his colleague, these companies were just as popular in Muslim and non-Muslim nations. He advised U.S.-based multinational corporations not to overreact to fears that America's sinking popularity will affect their bottom line, though he does recommend that they develop more senior executives who understand the Muslim world and that they bring Muslims onto their boards of directors.[7]

Consumer habits can be fickle, and it may not be entirely clear how America's popularity affects its major brands. The fortunes of individual American brands rise and fall, but certain longer-term trends are likely to continue. Consumers in Europe, and in Muslim Europe especially, may be increasingly drawn to products and services that reflect their core values, regardless of the brand name or country of origin. They will be making purchasing decisions not as a knee-jerk reaction to the power of multinationals, but rather as a statement about their lifestyles. Aside from the Muslim consumers who want to oppose American brands on political grounds, there are many more who simply seek products that reflect their Islamic values. Of course, sometimes both motivations may coexist for an individual consumer.

"A Beurger and a Qibla Cola—To Go"

Noor Saadeh, who co-created Razanne, complained about the presence of McDonald's in Mecca, but she might not object if it is replaced by a Muslim-made alternative. Halal meats are those prepared according to Islamic law. Like the ancient Jewish tradition of preparing kosher foods, meats are made halal based on the manner in which the animal is slaughtered, hung upside down to allow the blood to drain out. With the huge Muslim population in France, it was only a matter of time before entrepreneurs recognized the potential and opened a halal alternative. Beurger King Muslim looks and feels like the mainstream fast-food chain by a strikingly similar name, but this new restaurant in an eastern Paris suburb differs in substance. The name itself is a pun, a play on the French slang word *beur*, what a second-generation French North African is called. At Beurger King Muslim, not only are all meats prepared according to proper Islamic rituals and inspected three times daily, you can also watch a film on the life of the Prophet Mohammed on a flatscreen TV while you eat. The female employees may be veiled, and as you pay, the cash registers light up with the Arabic greeting *Salam Alakum*, or "peace be upon you." So far, business is booming, but the multinational giant Burger King has already been in touch via its attorneys. If BKM stays in business, it may begin offering alternative soft drinks to accompany its meals.[8]

"Think Before You Drink," implored the sign above the soft drink stand. When nearly 1 million Britons marched in London on February 15, 2003, to protest the United States' impending war on Iraq, marchers were handed bottles of a cola with a moral message. A few years ago, Tawfiq Mathlouthi, a Tunisian-born French-Muslim, awoke with a brainstorm. With so many Muslims spread across Europe, he saw he could make a fortune distributing Zam Zam Cola, an Iranian Coke competitor. But the Zam Zam makers turned him down. Undaunted, Mathlouthi found a recipe for cola on the Internet, cobbled together a few thousand dollars, and in late 2002 launched Mecca Cola. With a marketing flair and a keen sense of timing, Mathlouthi dubbed Mecca Cola official sponsor of the antiwar protests. According to Mathlouthi, Mecca Cola sold 3 million bottles within 10 months and grossed 3.6 million euros in 2003.[9] The company's aggressive expansion led it to Pakistan, where anti-Americanism runs feverishly high. After placing ads in local Pakistani newspapers for his own distributors—under the slogan, "No More Drinking Stupid. Drink With Commitment"—Mathlouthi received more than 1,000 responses.

Mecca Cola soon spawned its own rivals. Hoping to tap the same Muslim market, Qibla Cola, a British-based competitor, is targeting its soft drink line at "people of conscience everywhere." Under the banner, "Liberate Your Tastes," Qibla Cola began its sales in British towns with large Muslim populations, such as London, Derby, and Birmingham, but its success was so rapid that it now has distributors in Germany, Holland, Norway, and Luxembourg. The company is soon to penetrate India, Pakistan, Bangladesh, and Malaysia, and the company's executives aim to enter fifty other countries.

Like Mathlouthi, the founders of Qibla Cola also harbor serious qualms about American foreign policy. When I interviewed Abdul Hamid Ebrahim, the company's spokesman, he assured me that Qibla Cola is by no means anti-American. It is only opposed to U.S. policies, which they perceive as anti-Muslim. Some of his criticisms included American support for repressive regimes that restrict individual freedom and human rights; the overthrowing of regimes which are unwilling to cooperate with American business interests; American corporations' support for child labor in developing countries as a means of lowering labor costs and increasing profits; and the perceived corruption of awarding reconstruction contracts to Halliburton and other American firms.

The appeal of counter-American products is trickling down the continent to Turkey, where Cola Turka plans to wean Muslims off of Coke and Pepsi. Through a clever advertising campaign with Chevy Chase as its spokesman, the product gained national prominence nearly overnight. Television ads feature Chevy in Istanbul, unable to communicate in English. After a few swigs of Cola Turka, the comedian finds himself fluent in Turkish. One ad features Chevy with his family singing "Take Me Out to the Ballgame" until, after sipping Cola Turka, they uncontrollably burst into a Turkish national anthem. The message is not subtle: support the national soft drink, not the Americans. Coca Cola Turkey has been forced to slash its prices twice since Cola Turka's launch. Within just five months of the soft drink's introduction, it captured an astonishing 20 percent of the market. The product's success is spurred not simply by its taste. Opposition to American foreign policy runs high here: more than 90 percent of Turks were against the American invasion of Iraq.

Cracking the cola market is a notoriously tall order. Coke and

Pepsi predominate sales, controlling 60 percent of the West European soda market and 90 percent in the Middle East and North Africa. Coke alone sells 4 billion cases a year in Europe and the Middle East. Gifted marketing giant Richard Branson has tried for years to sap Coke and Pepsi's market shares with his Virgin Cola, to little avail. But the industry is so potentially profitable that gaining even a tiny percentage of the market can prove rewarding.

Some analysts believe that even if Mecca Cola or its rivals succeed and genuinely disrupt the current cola balance of power, Coke or Pepsi will simply buy the company, as they did with an earlier Indian rival, Thumbs Up, which is still sold in India. But the Muslim-made colas may not be as easy to buy off. Mecca Cola has a mission beyond the bottom line. To prove it, the company donates 20 percent of its net profits to Muslim charities: half to Palestinian nongovernmental organizations and half to European-based agencies. And this is one of Mecca Cola's main selling points: it gives Muslims a chance to proactively help their co-religionists while simultaneously sticking it to American corporate giants. Simply buying a bottle gives you a high that Coke can't match—or so the marketing strategy suggests.

While Cola Turka exploits Turkish nationalism, Qibla Cola, Mecca Cola, and Razanne appeal to pan-Islamism. Razanne embodies Muslim values: modesty, piety, and humanity over consumption. She lacks Barbie's beach house, car, and countless array of material possessions. She volunteers in the community, assisting the sick and poor. Analogously, Qibla and Mecca Cola appeal to Islamic virtues of charity and compassion. Qibla Cola also donates 20 percent of its profits, much of which goes to Islamic Aid. The company's stated aim is to focus on poverty reduction worldwide, healthcare, education, and sanitation. More recently the company has toned down its sponsorship of Islamic Aid, hoping to be seen as donating to a range of charities, not strictly those benefiting Muslims. This decision, however, may be precisely the wrong business strategy to pursue.

What fuels sales of Qibla Cola, Razanne, and other specifically Muslim-made products is not simply ambi-Americanism. Their appeal is to the Islamic values these products reflect. Muslim businesses hold a trump card in their competition with non-Muslim brands when they attract those who believe that boycotting American products is a religious obligation.

Waging Economic Jihad

"You are a nation without principles or manners. Values and principles to you are something which you merely demand from others, not that which you yourself must adhere to."[10]

Bin Laden has written a letter to America. The above statement comes from a document published in 2002. In that missive, the author, presumed to be Bin Laden himself, harangues America for its immorality, presenting a list of complaints from the commoditization of women to environmental destruction, hypocrisy, and violence against Muslims. Bin Laden warns the United States to either clean up its values or "expect us in New York and Washington." The document could easily be dismissed as the ravings of a zealot if it did not reflect some of the common critiques that moderate, religious Muslims make against America, and for that matter, against Europe as well.

The average moderate European Muslim rejects Bin Laden's violent tactics, but many share his perspective on the need to oppose American economic might. This is in part due to political reasons to oppose U.S. foreign policy, and in part, to reject the values that American goods are perceived to embody. In a 1990 speech, Bin Laden remarked: "When we buy American goods, we are accomplices in the murder of Palestinians. American companies make millions in the Arab world with which they pay taxes to the American government. The United States uses that money to send $3 billion a year to Israel, which it uses to kill Palestinians."[11]

Bin Laden's sentiments are sometimes echoed on English-language Islamic websites, which express a visceral resentment of

Israel, and by association, the United States. In April 2004, the portal IslamOnline posted several fatwas explaining that Muslims have a responsibility to wage "economic jihad" against American and Zionist businesses. Described as a prominent Muslim scholar, Sheikh Youssef Al-Qaradawi, declared that all monies used to purchase American and Zionist goods "eventually becomes bullets to be fired at the hearts of brothers and children in Palestine." He continued:

> American goods, exactly like "Israeli" goods, are forbidden. It is also forbidden to advertise these goods. America today is a second Israel. It totally supports the Zionist entity. The usurper could not do this without the support of America. "Israel's" unjustified destruction and vandalism of everything has been using American money, American weapons, and the American veto. America has done this for decades without suffering the consequences of any punishment or protests about their oppressive and prejudiced position from the Islamic world. The time has come for the Muslim umma to say "NO" to America, "NO" to its companies, and "NO" to its goods, which swamp our markets.

IslamOnline airs many voices of discontent with America. Al-Qaradawi maintains that Muslims commit a major sin not only when buying American or Zionist goods, but also by patronizing companies which support the Americans and Zionists, whatever that company's national origin. He gives the British-owned department store Marks and Spencer as one example.[12]

Another fatwa by Sheikh Faysal Mawlawi, deputy chairman of Al-Qaradawi's European Council for Fatwa and Research, supports a general boycott of American, British, and Zionist goods because of their "avowed enmity to Islam, Muslims, and Arabs." Sheikh Abdel Khaliq Hasan Ash-Shareef goes beyond Palestine to justify a boycott. "In light of the US-led war against Iraq, boycotting products of the US and its allies is a religious obligation upon all Muslims."[13]

On numerous other Web pages many angry voices can be heard. What they reveal is a palpable sense of Muslim embattlement within the secular, Western world. And the more aggressively that American secular values invade their daily lives, the more ferocious the resistance grows. Another popular site is IslamicAwakening.com, a site that emphasizes understanding Islam but which also discusses current events. One article the site posted calls for the boycotting of all businesses that support the "racist, Zionist state of Israel." The authors spotlight specific British businesses for targeting: Sainsbury's, Tescos, and Marks and Spencer stores. "The time has now come for the Muslims around the World to prove whether they are really sincere in their love and support of their Muslim brothers and sisters in Palestine."[14] It is difficult to say how wide the appeal of these cyber-fatwas is across Europe. Mahsa, the 26-year-old Iranian-born British woman with a doctorate from Oxford profiled in chapter 2, tells me that she has boycotted Marks and Spencer for years. One reason she decided to return to Iran to work was because she did not want to pay taxes that support British foreign policies, particularly those regarding Israel. Mahsa, remember, is a sober scientist, not prone to fanaticism or irrational hatreds.

Second-Circle Shoppers

In the introduction, I referred to Richard Clarke's concentric-circle metaphor, where the outermost circle represents the world's 1.3 billion Muslims and the innermost circle stands for the tiny number of violent extremists. Within the middle ring, the second circle, are the millions of Muslims who harbor deep ambivalence toward America and Europe. I have been arguing that this ambivalence is rooted in a discomfort with perceived mainstream values. At times their ambivalence manifests itself in protests over foreign policies that are seen to reflect un-Islamic values—policies that show insufficient concern for the poor, the disadvantaged, or the oppressed. At other times their ambivalence is expressed in buying patterns. Uneasy with the perceived values embodied in mainstream products, and wishing to support Muslim-made goods, they are seeking out alternatives. Razanne is one example of a values-driven product, but there are others.

Zaid's (formerly Caravan Saray) offers secure, online shopping for a wide range of Islamic and Muslim-made goods, from prayer rugs to beauty care, and much, much more. Their stated mission is "to market products developed and manufactured by Muslims throughout the world." By integrating people, tradition, and technology, "we help our customers maintain their Islamic identity while at the same time bridge the gap between traditional Islamic culture and the west."

Zaid's operates all their business transactions according to sharia law. Among their advertised selling points is their effort to keep Islamic etiquette with their Creator first, their stakeholders second. They support Islamic education through philanthropy and volunteering. They pay their suppliers and workers competitive wages promptly, as they are commanded to "pay the worker before his sweat dries." All products must be aesthetically pleasing, because "Allah is Beautiful and loves beauty." And perhaps most notably, they are committed to supporting independent manufacturers of Islamic goods.[15] In other words, buying products from Zaid's will support small Muslim businesses, not American multinational corporations.

TalkIslam's online store is a competitor to Zaid's. Based in Columbia, Maryland, this site offers a wide range of Islamic products at discount prices. It sells everything from perfumes to housewares, children's toys, and the latest electronics. One such device is a digital Quran, allowing the faithful to keep the entire holy book in their pocket for audio prayers or text displays. TalkIslam also sells numerous videos—educational Islamic lectures, documentaries, and films about Muslim issues. One popular film is *Brothers and Others: The Impact of 9/11 on Arabs, Muslims and South Asians in America*. Other films include *Man-Made Laws vs. Sharia: Ruling by*

Laws Other than What Allah Revealed, Gender Relations: Issues Facing Men and Women in Islam, and *The Empire and the Crescent: Global Implications for a New American Century.* Beyond educational and political films, the site also sells videos on mental health, such as *Islam's Treatment for Anxiety and Worry.*

Yet another shopping portal, SoundVision.com, aims to do more than provide Islamic goods. Based in Chicago, SoundVision presents itself as a hub for Islamic media. Asserting that, "the attitudes and behavior of men and women today are shaped and molded by the media whose ideals and images, by and large, are non-Islamic," SoundVision seeks "to produce content with Islamic ideals and images." One such product is RadioIslam.com, a talk radio discussion forum for issues of concern to the umma. The company also produces the 14-part film series, "Adam's World," entertaining and educational children's videos featuring Adam, an orange-colored puppet boy, and his many friends, whose adventures teach Islamic values.

Internet portals such as these are filling physical, spiritual, and mental needs for growing numbers of diaspora Muslims. They are enabling Muslims to be modern consumers in Western societies, but to do so on their own terms. They are engaging in economic jihad, though not in the sense of waging war on the infidel. No doubt some have heeded the call of IslamOnline's fatwas to boycott American- and Zionist-supporting firms. But many others are waging a greater jihad—the struggle within themselves to follow the straight path. Part of that struggle is to resist a perceived empty and materialistic culture. Muslim enterprises are providing an opportunity for Muslims to feel better about the products they purchase.

The product possibilities are themselves expanding. In 2003, LG Electronics, Inc., South Korea's second-largest cell phone manufacturer, introduced a mobile phone—but with a clever new feature. In addition to its wide screen, compass, and location-tracking software, the LG-G5300 also includes a Qibla pointer:

it automatically identifies the direction of Mecca, toward which Muslims pray. Also that year Mannesmann, a division of Siemens, applied for a patent on a similar device for automobile drivers to see Mecca's precise location while on the road. The system will even automatically play the call to prayer at the appropriate hour.

The Gulf-based meat-packaging company Co-op, the most popular name in halal meats throughout the Gulf States, has for the first time begun selling its products in England, hoping to capture Britain's hungry Muslim market. And that market is not inconsequential. Although British Muslims comprise only about 3 percent of the population, they consume an estimated 20 percent of all lamb and mutton.[16] Finding halal meats has become increasingly complex in the age of genetically modified foods and feeds. If animals are raised on feed tainted with meat, the animal cannot be considered halal, even if it is slaughtered in the prescribed fashion. This is one of the controversies surrounding the Al Safa meat company, a Canadian-based firm that supplies halal meats in North America. The fact that the firm is owned by Jews, Henry and David Muller, a father-and-son partnership, also has some Muslims up in arms.[17]

Banks are also cashing in on the Muslim market. Because the charging of interest is strictly forbidden by the Quran, Europe's Muslims, until recently, have not had any banking options that met their religious requirements. In 2003, the Islamic Bank of Britain became the first bank to offer sharia-compliant services. I described in chapter 1 the shiny new branch of IBB that opened across from the East London mosque. Now, in a sign of Muslims' growing relevance to British society and economy, HSBC bank has created an Islamic financial services division. The division, headed by Iqbal Khan, is targeting Britain's 340,000 Muslim households with their combined estimated savings of $1 billion. Other estimates suggest that Britain has more than 5,000 Muslim millionaires, with liquid assets of nearly 3.6 billion pounds.[18] Lloyds Bank offers a personal bank account for Muslim clients. Barclays Bank is likely to follow in the quest to capture a market whose value is estimated at between $200 billion and $300 billion worldwide, and growing at a rate of 15 percent annually. Andrew Buxton, the former head of Barclays Bank, chairs a working group within the Bank of England. Buxton's mission is to create sharia-compliant financial products, including mortgages and insurance plans.[19] Beyond Britain, the German state of Saxony-Anhalt launched in 2004 a €100 million, sharia-compliant bond. Banks are eager to attract Muslim clients, and if successful, it is likely that they will expand operations to France, Holland, and other parts of Europe with sizeable Muslim populations.

Muslim investors also have an online option. Through Islamiq-money.com, launched in 2000, Muslims can access financial services of all kinds with the knowledge that transactions are conducted and businesses are adhering to sharia, and the online services are vast, including debt consolidation, refinancing, cash advances, mortgages, credit repair, credit cards, credit reports, auto loans, money management, insurance, and fundraising assistance. You can also purchase healthcare products, cars, homes, computers, gifts, flowers, music, electronics, cell phones, cruises, airline tickets, dental plans, weight- and hair-loss products, and even explore online dating.[20]

Wealthy investors and middle-class entrepreneurs are not the only Muslims eager to find sharia-compliant financial products. Muslim students in Britain have struggled with the problem of taking out student loans, since those loans are charged interest. Members of the Federation of Student Islamic Societies have even gone as far as to argue their case before Britain's Education Secretary, urging him to support the creation of Muslim-friendly student loans.[21] The issue of student loans is of critical importance to some of Europe's younger Muslims who see standard Western banking procedures as a barrier to their educations.

Below are the words of one (presumably young) convert to Islam, arguing forcefully against liberal interpretations of sharia.

The author first describes how Muslim scholars had encouraged the taking of loans as a means to an end. The writer then links the use of credit cards to passivity over the plight of the umma.

> He taught me that the rules in Islam are very flexible, like the Christianity I had just left. I now believed that I could interpret them to suit my needs. Under this understanding, anyone can use interest for anything he/she "thinks" is necessary. So, when I thought it was necessary to own a car, or I could not get to work, I took a loan. It also made me understand that all the credit cards I had were OK 'cause I needed them. The reality was that I did not need the car, I could have taken a bus; I did not need the cards, I could have been patient, I did not need anything because my life was never in danger, but I had been taught that necessity in Islam was defined by what I considered necessary. This led me to inadvertently commit many sins that put me "at war" with Allah. . . .
>
> Our "scholars" are constantly trying to make things easier on us, telling us it's OK to wear a headpiece with pants and call it hijab, saying it is okay to shave or trim the beard, saying it is acceptable to go to that social gathering at work even though alcohol is being served because we will lose our jobs if we don't, saying it is okay to sell alcohol or pork as long as we do not touch it or consume it, saying it is okay to take a house loan because we need to establish a base in this country, saying it is okay to have a credit card 'cause we need it in case we want to rent a car or in the case of an emergency . . . the list is endless. . . .
>
> What will we say to Allah when He questions us about our brothers and sisters in Kosovo, Somalia, Sudan, Kashmir, Palestine, Bosnia, Algeria, Ethiopia, Lebanon, India etc.? . . . What will we say when He questions us about our credit cards, our school loans our houses and even masjids [mosques] built from riba [money that has earned interest]?[22]

Taken individually, the developments described above—a modest Muslim Barbie, Muslim-made colas, sharia-friendly banks, or

Internet shopping portals—might seem insignificant. But viewed as a whole, a meaningful trend emerges. More than just the corporate bottom line is at stake in the current clash of the Barbies. The rise of Islamic goods and services is a powerful expression of both a rising ambi-Americanism and a growing religiosity among Europe's younger Muslims. The challenge to profits is marginal; the challenge to mainstream consumer values is real.

Chapter 7

NEW EUROPE,
SAME OLD ISSUES

If New Europe were to showcase a country, Slovenia would be it. This tiny country of 2 million inhabitants lies south of Austria, east of Italy, and northwest of former Yugoslavia. Over the course of the last few centuries Slovenes have fallen under the dominion of Italian princedoms, been subjects of the Habsburg monarchy, and members of a southern Slav confederacy. Following World War I, Slovenes were merged into a country called the Kingdom of Serbs, Croats, and Slovenes, a name that gives some idea of its sense of national unity. In 1929, the kingdom was renamed Yugoslavia, meaning literally "southern Slavs." When the Balkan wars erupted in 1993, triggering the breakup of Yugoslavia, Slovenia saw just ten days of fighting before it declared its neutrality and its independence.

Today, at long last, Slovenia is a country in its own right, intent on a steady closening with the West. Spared the devastation of war that savaged Bosnia, Serbia, and Croatia, Slovenia has upgraded its economy, modernized its infrastructure, and in May 2004 joined the European Union. Now the EU flag flies prominently throughout the capital.

Slovenia is in many respects a model of what the rest of New Europe would like to be. In the capital, Ljubljana, steepled churches line clean and orderly cobblestone streets. High Baroque buildings flank the river, which runs through the center of town. A Germanic efficiency seems effortlessly balanced by a relaxed Mediterranean lifestyle. Locals sip coffee at outdoor cafés across from tourists checking email at Internet cafés. Steep, wooded hillsides and a medieval castle are visible from the city center. Were it not for the Slavic words on shop windows, you might guess you were in Austria.

Slovenia's government is a stable parliamentary democracy whose leaders have worked hard to reform institutions and adopt European standards. In 2004, it became the first transition country to change from being a borrower to a donor nation in the World Bank. Its progressive outlook even led it to adopt gay-rights legislation, something unheard of in the rest of the Balkan states. Given Slovenia's forward-looking nature, if Muslims cannot make it here, their prospects in the restive New Europe may be dim.

For the past three decades, Slovenia's Muslims have been struggling to erect a genuine mosque in the capital, but opposition has been strong. More than twenty proposed sites have been rejected on the grounds that a dome and minarets would not fit with the rest of the city's architecture. But ethnic Slovenian opposition rests on more than just aesthetics. The country is predominantly Catholic, and Muslims constitute approximately 2.5 percent of the population. Slovenes opposed to the mosque gathered more than 11,000 signatures and pressed the city government to block its construction. The Archbishop of Ljubljana allegedly even remarked that a mosque is a political center, whereas a church is a religious one. Slovenia's chief Muslim authority, Mufti Osman Djogic, swiftly countered that such assertions were based on prejudice and misconceptions.[1]

Down a quiet, unassuming residential street about a mile outside the capital's center sits a modest four-story house. From the outside it looks no different from any of the other homes in a neighborhood. And that is for good reason. For this is the only mosque in Ljubljana, and neighbors do not want it to be a visible presence.

Sulat was born in Bosnia. Like the vast majority of Slovenia's 50,000 Muslims, he came from Bosnia as an economic migrant seeking work. And like so many economic migrants across Europe, he settled in the new country and raised a family. Now in his mid-50s, he gives no outward clues that he is a Muslim. His 5'6" frame is clad in long, tan hiking shorts and a dark blue rugby shirt. His light eyes, silver hair, and trim figure accentuate a healthy glow. He welcomes my two friends and me into the mosque.

Suleiman, an older gentleman in his seventies, is not the imam, but he is looking after the mosque while the imam is away on vacation. His black leather shoes are worn. His face is lined and weathered. He also stands about 5'6" tall, has dark brown eyes, a deeply lined forehead, and a warm smile. Unlike Sulat, Suleiman was born in Ljubljana, though he is also of Bosnian descent. Although the majority of Slovenia's Muslims are Bosnian, the country is also home to Muslims from Turkey, Iraq, Palestine, and Egypt; many have come for work and others to study.

"Muslims are democratic," Suleiman says. "We welcome all people no matter where they are from. But the Slovenes . . . " He pauses. I smile and nod, encouraging him to speak his mind. He continues, "Slovenes are fearful of foreigners. They think our treatment of women is terrible, but here women can pray alongside men."

To prove it, they invite us into the central prayer room, shaking the hand of my female friend. It is a small, circular room, covered in ornate carpets. Pictures of famous mosques adorn the walls, juxtaposed to glass plate etchings of elaborate Arabic script.

"Have you experienced any direct hostility from the neighbors?" I ask.

"The people here are not extremists," Sulat says. "They just don't want us to build minarets or be too visible. They just don't know anything about Islam or Muslims."

Muslims in Slovenia faced strong opposition to the building of any mosques larger than the one we currently stand in. The prayer room is designed to accommodate only 50 worshippers comfortably, but it must hold two hundred men and women, pressed shoulder to shoulder. Suleiman says the city's Muslim community needs three or four more mosques to serve the entire congregation.

After leaving the mosque, Sulat invites us to his home to meet his wife and son. He asks us to wait in the street before entering: "I have a dog," he says. We cannot quite figure out why his owning a dog should require us to wait across the street, but then we hear it. Yelps, barks, and savage, snarling sounds ring out from the backyard. Sulat is shouting something in Bosnian, the meaning of which I can only guess. We hear the sounds of a heavy metal chain being dragged through the gravel at high speed. More yelping, more shouting, and the commotion goes on for several minutes. "I'm sure it will be fine," I tell my friends, more to reassure myself than them.

Sulat opens the gate and welcomes us in. The dog's chain is just long enough that if we stay to the right on the path to his door, a good foot or two separates us from the pet. "He's harmless," Sulat laughs, as he escorts us upstairs. We remove our shoes, as we do before entering any Muslim home or mosque.

Sulat's wife shakes our hands and greets us warmly, ushering us into the living room, where we are surrounded by paintings of mosques in Sarajevo and Istanbul. While we chat, Sulat brings us a beautiful leather-bound copy of the Quran printed in both Bosnian and Arabic. His wife hurriedly brings us coffee and tea. Their son, a tall man in his early thirties who works in a local restaurant and lives with his parents, joins us. Sulat's second son is married to a Catholic Slovenian woman. They have a home not far away. Today, Sulat and his wife are looking after Aysha, their granddaughter, an adorable four-year-old with whom they speak in Bosnian.

"You've lived in Ljubljana for almost thirty years. Do you feel like you fit in well with your neighbors?" I ask.

"Slovenians are a bit cold," Sulat observes. "They don't really have the temperament for foreigners. In Bosnia, people care much more whether you're a kind person, not what religion you are."

"Why do you think they don't have the temperament for Muslims?" I ask him.

"They think that if too many of us come here, we'll multiply, and then we will overwhelm them."

Slovenia is a microcosm of the problems Muslims are facing across Europe. Many ethnic Europeans fear the swelling numbers of Muslims in their midst. They oppose overt, prominent displays of Islam in their cities and try to ban mosques with minarets or domes. They understand little about Islam, and since the terror attacks on the West beginning with 9/11, their Islamophobia has been on the rise.

There is a fear among some Europeans that Islam is not compatible with Europe's democratic ways. This is why Mustafa Yoldaş, the Muslim community leader in Hamburg described in chapter 3, has devoted hours to speaking engagements reassuring Germans that Islam and democracy are compatible. I had not met a European Muslim who believed that Islam and democracy could not coexist—until I came to Prague.

I had just stepped out of my hotel to explore the city when, within five minutes, a fully covered woman approached me asking for directions to a local restaurant. I then noticed that she was with a number of other Muslims, or so it appeared from their outer garb. I took this as a good omen that my official encounters with Muslims would come with ease. During the next several days I continued to notice a surprising number of Muslim tourists wandering the streets, just as I was doing. Prague is a popular tourist spot, and with good reason. Its mixture of impressive architecture, extraordinary food, and rich history, not to mention still affordable prices, draws thousands of visitors each year. But I had come to meet Muslims who live in the Czech Republic, not Muslim tourists.

Down a nondescript, noisy road in a commercial district just beyond the historic center sits an average, modern shopping mall. This time, if the signs were not in Czech, you might think you were in Houston, Denver, or any other major American city. But if you take an unmarked set of stairs just one story above the mall, you will find a small, converted office space. Here is the Islamic Community Center of Prague, inhabiting just four rooms. One room serves as a library. Another spartan, carpeted, rectangular space is the prayer room. A cramped office with a single computer comprises the administrative center.

"Welcome, brother." Rafiq offers me his hand. "Anything you want to know, I am an open book for you."

Rafiq is a 24-year-old mechanical engineering student from Saudi Arabia. He wears a thick black beard that offsets his youthful energy. His intense enthusiasm for Islam is apparent as we speak. Like Mustafa in Hamburg, Mahsa in London, and many other young Muslims I have met, it was in Europe that Rafiq became a true believer. "I had wrecked my stomach with alcohol," he recalls. "I wanted girls, drugs, anything to fill the void." As an unemployed young man in his homeland, there was quite a large void to fill. "In Saudi Arabia boys don't have much to do except play football and hang out."

Rafiq's father had once studied in Germany and felt that his son would greatly benefit from studying abroad as well. So at age 21, Rafiq arrived in Prague. One afternoon a friend was downloading some Quranic songs off the Internet and something clicked inside of Rafiq. Suddenly he wanted to know more about Islam.

Soon after he began his Islamic inquiry, Rafiq abandoned his reckless ways and completely changed his lifestyle. He married that same year. "If you're a young guy and you want to have sex," he smiles, "Islam has an answer: get married." In fact, for Rafiq, Islam gave him all the answers he sought. Today he helps to run the Islamic Community Center, which is one of only two Muslim centers in Prague. The community is small, he tells me, and few people come to the center to pray daily. "The Czech people do not like any religions, but especially not Islam. And that is a shame for the Czechs, because the society's values are not helpful to people."

"Why do you say that?"

Rafiq pauses to reflect, as if scanning his databanks for an appropriate anecdote. "One time, before I was married, I met a Czech girl. We sat and talked and I started to ask her about her family, and suddenly she began to cry. I thought she was going to tell me that her father beat her or something like that. Instead, she said she couldn't believe that I cared about her family because it was not something that men usually asked her about. You see," Rafiq explains, "in Western societies men use women like cigarettes. They take one, enjoy her, and throw her away when they are done. And then they take another. Islam teaches us to respect all women and to treat them like our sisters and mothers. After all, they are someone's sister or mother."

"So what do you think about the attacks in London a few weeks ago?" I ask, referring to the July 7, 2005, suicide bombings. "Could something like that ever happen here?"

"I don't think so," Rafiq smiles, "we are not important enough here. And what do the Czech people have to do with Iraq?"

"Do you think the attacks are directed against America and Britain because of their role in Iraq?"

"Of course. Saddam was a very bad man, but you punished Iraqi children for years with sanctions. We like the idea of freedom, but we think you mean something different by it." And then he adds, "America is the enemy of Islam." Possibly noticing my expression, he quickly continues, "I have no problems with Americans themselves. We are friends here." I am glad to hear this, but concerned by what follows. "America is the enemy just as much as the Saudi government. Both are against true Islam. Both oppose justice, and both must change."

Rafiq tells me that all the worshippers in Prague are peaceful people, especially the imam. Unfortunately, he still experiences discrimination in his daily life. One of his engineering professors refers to him in front of the class as "Rafiq bin Laden." But Rafiq does not seem bitter in any respect. If anything, he exudes a hopeful, positive energy.

Rafiq wants me to meet some of the female worshippers gathering in a prayer room. Some of them are recent Czech converts. Tereza, now known as Fatima, converted only a few months ago. She is 16 and in an abusive situation at home. Her family, she says, drinks alcohol as if it were their hobby. Just yesterday she left her family's house and moved in with one of the women in the congregation. Her parents called her a bitch and other names she could not repeat. Like all the women in this Islamic Center, only her face and hands are showing. Another female convert says that she started out wanting to know why Islam was such a bad religion. The more she learned about it, however, the more she came to believe in it. Rafiq says that most of the converts he meets in Prague are women.

I ask Rafiq if he thinks sharia should be the law in Europe. He does not answer directly. "I'd like to see it first come to the Muslim lands," he replies. "Islam gives us many rules to live by, and these rules are good for all people. What we do not want is democracy."

I'm surprised to hear him say this, since most of the Muslims I speak with across Europe think democracy is a good system, as long as Muslims themselves are able to participate in it. But Rafiq has a different view. "In democracies, any group with enough influence can get its way. For example, we don't think that gay relationships should be permitted. In democracy, these kinds of relationships are being condoned."

It sounds like Rafiq opposes democracy because the majority might adopt laws counter to his interpretation of Islam, which makes me suspect that he very much would prefer to see sharia be the law of the land in Europe. As prayer time is about to begin, I thank Rafiq for his openness and his time, and we agree to keep in touch by email.

Muslim and Gay

I want to take a brief detour from New Europe to visit an issue lurking behind the values question. Among the repeated calls for greater social justice that I hear from across Muslim Europe, homosexuality remains a constant sticking point. Mainstream European society has accommodated gays and lesbians by affording them equal protection under the law. Most European states have anti-discrimination legislation to protect homosexuals. In June 2005, Spain became the third nation, after the Netherlands and Belgium, to allow gay marriage. But gay marriage is not open for discussion among most of Europe's Muslims. On one extreme are those who have called for gays to be stoned to death, as mentioned in chapter 4. While such violence is not the norm, Muslims like Rafiq are strongly opposed to enhancing gay rights. Mustafa Yoldaş says he cannot possibly condone homosexuality, as the Quran is clear on the issue. With so much apparent consensus on the issue within Muslim Europe, I thought it would be interesting to talk with a gay Muslim.

"They always fixate on this one issue. They're obsessed with homosexuality." Abdul is an Arab man who works in London, where there is an active and vibrant gay population. Nonetheless, the coming-out process for him has been long and difficult. "I don't think you realize that if my family back home were to find out, my life would be at risk," he explains, and he is not exaggerating. Abdul comes from a rural area where honor killings still occur. Only a few years ago a young girl in his home region became pregnant out of wedlock. Her mother and siblings saw her belly growing larger each day, but they told her father that she was just getting fat. On the day she gave birth, they kept the father away from the home and then tried to hide the baby in a neighbor's house. When the father discovered what was happening, he asked no questions.

He simply went to the kitchen, found a large butcher's knife, and slit his daughter's throat. When the court later ruled on the case, the father was exonerated because, according to local customs, he was defending his family's honor. Abdul believes that a worse fate would befall him if they knew he was gay.

Most Muslims I know tell me that homosexuality is a sin. The Quran cites the Old Testament tale of Sodom and Gomorrah, and some point to that passage as proof of Islam's condemnation of homosexual acts. IslamOnline even has a "cyber counseling" section where people write in to ask advice on personal issues. I showed Abdul the site's comments on homosexuality.

Jawed, a 22-year-old Dutch Muslim, writes in about his struggle with homosexual tendencies. He explains that on the inside he feels like a girl, though on the outside he looks like a boy. He has felt attracted to boys since he was nine, and now he pleads for help. He has prayed to God, but nothing changes. The online counselor explains that homosexuality results from poor upbringing and arrested development. "The current misguided understanding is that homosexual people are born that way. There is no conclusive scientific evidence for this assumption; this assumption is guided by political reasoning to justify homosexual behavior. . . . Unguided fantasies and feelings, left without serious thought into Islam, will place stronger emphasis in following our basal needs to satisfy those triggers of sexual desire." The counselor suggests keeping "a strong bond with a pious masculine Muslim man to help guide him about the way a man should behave."

"Abdul, you are a devout Muslim. You pray five times daily, you do charitable works helping the needy, you observe the Ramadan fast. How do you reconcile your homosexuality with your religion?"

"I believe that God does not make mistakes. Since God made me this way, there must be a reason for it that I cannot understand. But God also never gives us a burden that we cannot bear, even though at times our challenges may seem too much. God believes in us. As far as the Quran goes, there are also parts of it that suggest to me that homosexuality is not a sin. You have to see the book as a whole, not just lift a sentence here and there to suit your needs or support a particular argument."

Abdul considers himself a good Muslim. His boyfriend, who is also a European of Arab descent, works in London as well. On the surface, the two seem like well-integrated, contented, religious European Muslims. And yet they feel tremendous pressure to remain closeted among their Muslim colleagues and associates. This raises the question of how accepting and tolerant Europe's younger Muslims will be of homosexuals as they increasingly enter the political process.

Back to New Europe

As with the rest of the EU, the number of Muslims residing within the ten newly acceded states (Cyprus, the Czech Republic, Estonia, Hungary, Latvia, Lithuania, Malta, Poland, Slovakia, and Slovenia) is difficult to pinpoint primarily because of illegal immigration. The rough estimate stands at around 300,000. The greatest number are concentrated in Cyprus, with around 140,000, or approximately 18 percent (see Appendix for further detail).

The challenges for New Europe in integrating its Muslim residents are potentially even more serious than for the larger and wealthier EU members. Integration measures involve state spending. Language-training courses, for example, are typically funded by the state. Even if the level of Muslim migrants does not rise (which seems unlikely, given that the demographic pressures are similar in New Europe to the rest of the EU), the newly acceded countries will have to devote resources to prevent a growing Muslim underclass from forming, as has happened in France and Holland.

Several cultural issues will need to be finessed. Whereas Britain and France have permitted mosques to spring up where desired, Germany and other EU states have placed some restrictions on mosques. The Muezzin's call to worship—the sonorous tones of Quranic passages sung at prayer times, usually over a megaphone for all the neighborhood to hear—has to date been banned in Germany. Neighbors object that it disturbs the peace; however, the hourly church bell chimes are not considered a disturbance. If Slovenia's case is indicative, countries that are predominantly monocultures with high ethnic homogeneity will oppose a visible Muslim presence. Again, such policies can only be sustained if the Muslim minority remains small and of limited political power, neither of which conditions seems likely to last for long.

In contrast, America has quietly become one of the most openly multi-religious nations in the world. Hindu temples, Buddhist shrines, and Muslim mosques now pepper the cityscapes from coast to coast. So far, this has not brought discord or unrest, but in Europe, where the context is quite different, the results could be destabilizing.

What will happen to the face of Europe in just twenty years, when Muslim birthrates and immigration levels have swollen to make Muslim populations sizeable minorities in Europe's historically Christian capitals? Will mosques coexist peacefully alongside churches? Would neighborhoods become multi-ethnic, as in London's Bethnal Green? Will Muslim workers enjoy the same opportunities as their non-Muslim peers?

Given the European Muslim dynamics that have been presented thus far, imagine what the future could look like from a European Muslim perspective. What might a typical day be like for one young, religious Muslim woman, in the year 2025?

Chapter 8

THE FUTURE
OF MUSLIM EUROPE

Aisha woke up crying. She lay motionless on her side in bed, her knees drawn close to her chest. These were the critical moments, the chance to grasp and hang onto the fleeting images that only seconds ago had consumed her. But the stark light of consciousness scattered those remnants beyond her mental reach. All that remained was a queasiness in her gut and a vague sense of being watched. But she knew that this was impossible. Aisha was always alone.

The air inside her room was still. Her nightclothes were wet and sticky. A gentle rain tapped upon the skylight above her bed. For a few moments she watched the droplets trickle down the slanted pane. She rose, showered and dressed, then knelt for her morning prayers. The rhythmic tones of the Muezzin's call to prayer echoed down the Sultan Strasse, reverberating from mosque to mosque across Berlin. When Aisha finished her prayers, she removed the hand-held QuickLink from inside her gown to receive the day's assignments. Across the screen flashed the date: June 1, 2025. A fleeting smile passed across her face. This month marked the tenth anniversary of the League's founding. She felt proud of what they had built in that time, but overwhelmed by the tasks that lay ahead.

"Salam Alakum, und guten Morgen, Aisha." Mirar Erdemli's plumpish, three-dimensional figure appeared within the QuickLink

viewing screen. Mirar's image, recorded the night before, ran down the list of homes Aisha was to visit. Erdinç needed numbing tablets for the pain in his throat. Devrim's children needed new shoes. Feyzi's family needed food. All were families she knew well. All were party members. And though it often pained her to see so many brothers and sisters in need, she took comfort in knowing she could help to ease their troubles. And she knew she was building the party with every home visitation.

None in the party was as respected as Mirar, for few could claim they were present at the creation when the Pan-Islamic League first assembled in Marseilles. Mirar was one of the Party's founding 200, and she had selflessly devoted herself to the PIL's program ever since.

Aisha half listened to Mirar's list. There were eight home visitations in all, and one visit to the Residents in Wellness Center D. If she spent an hour with each, including travel time, it would be a tiring day. She snapped shut the QuickLink as she rose, placed a few chocolate pieces in her purse for the youngest Kattab boy, and headed for the door. In the hallway she slipped into her flat gray walking shoes, but realized she had forgotten her biometric identification card. Thanks to the PIL's lobbying efforts in Brussels, Muslims were exempted from the requirement to have the BICs inserted into the ankle, although the penalties for not presenting one's BIC if stopped by Defenders were severe. Slipping out of her shoes, she stepped back into her bedroom and placed the tiny silver disc into her purse.

Aisha's steps were hurried, her breathing fast. She walked along the Kanal Strasse, her nostrils curled. Though Kreuzberg's streets nearly always stank of rotting garbage, most days she never noticed it. But this morning the odors struck her as especially rank. The masjid trash collection teams were behind schedule this month. Again too few neighbors had paid their dues and the garbage had been piling up behind stores, homes, and restaurants. She passed a cluster of rats gnawing at a garbage heap. A few small children were washing themselves in the canal's filthy waters on her left, while other children kicked a sagging football back and forth. The trees that lined the canal's banks were darkened with a blackish gray dust. Farther down the road, she passed Pasha's Clothing Store, where the heavy smell of charred embers still drifted down the block. They had lost half their store in a fire last week. It took more than two hours for the untrained masjid emergency squad to quench the flames with what few blankets and buckets they could gather. Despite the passing days, she could still feel the lingering smoke against her cheeks. A black taste settled on her tongue.

Her first stop would have to be Ali's Produce. A windowless storefront concealed from view a wealth of unmodified fruits and vegetables. Aisha did not have to knock. Her approach was announced to Ali at least a minute before she arrived. His cameras scanned the faces of all passersby. Since she was a regular, they had her image in the system. The titanium door slid aside and noiselessly sealed behind her as she stepped inside. Ali's business was one of the few that continued to thrive no matter whether economic conditions rose or fell.

"Meribe. Guten Morgen, Aisha," Ali smiled, his squat, burly body lumbering up the aisle to greet her. He bowed slightly at her. "The usual?" he asked. Aisha nodded and forced a smile in return. Ali turned and began loading a bag with oranges, bananas, and other smallish, slightly imperfect but naturally grown fruits. The Greens were right about one thing, Aisha thought. The modified food that most Europeans ate was unnatural and un-Godly.

"Have you seen the news?" Ali asked, handing her several sacks of produce across the counter. Frau Pallaci is addressing Parliament again." Ali touched a finger to his wristwatch and the viewing wall lit up. The bulbous cheeks of Ariana Pallaci filled the screen, her white hair reflecting off the spotlights, her smooth, unnatural skin glistening as she spoke. Aisha turned her face to the ground, but she could not help herself from listening a little longer to the White Tigress, the woman who, with no official governmental position, largely ruled the lives of millions.

"Parliament has failed to make good on its promises. Healthcare is in a state of decay. Seniors across Europe are barely surviving the mistakes of poorly-trained nurses' aides. Nearly 12 percent of elderly cannot afford the cost of pulmonary enhancement devices. Another 4 percent cannot afford. . . " Aisha could not listen. Her grip tightened on her grocery bags.

The selfishness! How could Pallaci speak of seniors' needs when across Europe children were hungry, sick, and homeless, largely because of her?

Controlling the largest voting bloc in Europe, Pallaci's power knew few bounds. A decade ago, when, at age 69, Pallaci gained control of the Pensioners' Party, she pledged cooperation and balance. But she lied. In those ten years she not only continued the policies of her predecessors, she also expanded them, ratcheting up her demands for seniors, draining away the bulk of taxes to her supporters, leaving ever fewer crumbs to be meted out for social services that existed only in name. "You will be one of us one day," she shouted in every election year. And how the craven politicians groveled for the slightest sign of her endorsement.[1]

Aisha was nearly at the exit when Pallaci's voice faded and the news anchor's soothing tones announced the next story. "Tragedy strikes Denmark. Sheikh Hasan Abdul al-Bani, Copenhagen's leading imam, was found dead in his home yesterday evening." Aisha wheeled around at the viewing wall. "Europol investigators have been silent on the cause of death, but EuroNews has learned that homicide detectives were called to the scene shortly after midnight. No further details have been released at this time. In other news, a decision by the Supreme Council of Greater Russia . . ."

Aisha stood motionless for a moment. Something in the video clip of Europol squads caught her eye. "Ali, could you replay that clip for me, please?"

Ali raised a bushy eyebrow slightly and obeyed. The image recurred, showing teams of police milling about in a narrow Copenhagen street. "Freeze that," Aisha snapped. "There, in the lower right corner. Can you zoom to that?" Ali fiddled with his wrist controls and a uniformed man appeared large on the screen.

"Defenders," Ali said with surprise. "You have a sharp eye, Aisha."

They looked like typical Europol investigators, but the light blue lightening-bolt insignia on their chests set them apart. But what would Defenders be doing on a murder case, especially the murder of another imam? It didn't make sense.

Ali saw the question contracting her expression. "There are many strange things these days, Aisha. If it doesn't concern you, it's best not to inquire."

Ali peered curiously at her. "Did you know al-Bani?" he asked, with a trace of genuine concern.

Aisha hesitated for a moment. "No." She paused. "I never met him." And then she added, "Thank you for asking." She gathered up her groceries and swiftly passed out into the busy, rainy street.

The Defenders worked for BlueBlood Securities, the sole private security agency in Europe. Their reach was great, manufacturing and controlling all surveillance equipment, the software that ran it, and the men who served it. BlueBlood also operated the Wellness Centers, where many young Muslim men were taken for their crimes. According to an agreement forged with the European Parliament, BlueBlood was granted broad police authority as a means of supplementing Europol's limited resources. Defenders were the frontline representatives, vested with the authority to carry arms, interrogate, and arrest suspected criminals. And although they swore oaths to uphold universal human rights, Muslims knew better. No Muslim could help fearing their approach.

Her mind was full of questions. Why would Defenders, who cared only about harassing Muslims, be assigned to the case of another murdered imam? Her heart sank. Somehow, though she'd no idea yet how, Aisha knew that her own fate was tied to al-Bani's. She could sense now that her troubles were just beginning.

Aisha returned to the Kanal Strasse and headed toward the S-Bahn. As she passed the neighborhood madrassa, she heard the school bell ring and watched the children file into the glistening new school to begin their studies. She felt proud about Madrassa 9, for she and the PIL had helped make it a shining point of hope for Kreuzberg's children. Aisha thought back to her own childhood, before Saudi beneficence had brought the madrassas into such abundance. It was another lifetime: a time before the Party, before Brussels, even before the GERA itself. She felt old at this moment. Painfully old. Had there truly been a time before the GERA.

No one much noticed it at the time. The media made little mention of it, and those who spoke out against it were portrayed as un-European.

It was one of those things that only in retrospect did people consider a turning point. Only later did people joke of living in "the modern GERA." Aisha was just a little girl when it all began.

The truth about the GERA was, of course, more complex, for the changes that followed the Great European Reform Act of 2012 were already underway long before. The GERA was not one act, but a series of legislative reforms undertaken around what was called the "Brussels consensus." It began innocuously enough with tax policy. A movement of industrialists and businesspeople across Europe had been pushing for a common EU tax policy that would lessen the burden on corporations and spur growth. Each success built on the last.

Soon their hand-picked and carefully groomed candidates gained a majority of seats in the European Parliament. Steadily they reduced taxes of all kinds, stimulating economic growth and making Europe a genuine engine of innovation and growth. The gross domestic products of all EU member states rose, and the wealth that individual businessmen accrued was spectacular, until at last, all corporate taxes were outlawed and entrepreneurs were granted special tax-free status on their personal earnings. It was argued that by unfettering the entrepreneurial members of society from burdensome taxes, they would be able to produce more, expand their businesses, create more jobs, and improve conditions for all. Wealth, they insisted, would slither down the social hierarchy to the benefit of all. Of course, there was opposition to the reforms, but the democratically elected Parliament continued to pass them, at first by narrow margins, but then with increasingly convincing majorities.

Concomitant with the tax reforms came a series of even bolder deregulation and privatization acts. With a shrinking tax base and the rising costs of healthcare for a rapidly aging population, businesses could not remain competitive in the global marketplace, it was argued. Europe's restrictive environmental regulations had to be relaxed. Individual European states could no longer afford as many of the social services they had once maintained, and it was believed that the private sector could provide those same services more efficiently, services like prisons, schools, fire departments, and police.

But as time passed, those private businesses, increasingly owned by fewer and fewer holding companies, found it unprofitable to operate in the poorer districts. Most of Kreuzberg's residents could not afford the trash collection fees and opted not to subscribe. With only one in ten homes in some neighborhoods as paying customers, garbage collection firms were losing money by servicing Kreuzberg and other poorer parts of Europe's major cities. The companies agreed that those neighborhoods should be granted the freedom to dispose of their own trash as they saw fit. A similar pattern evolved with fire departments, schools, and other services previously financed by the public sector.

Aisha boarded the crowded S-Bahn at Kotbussertor and sank into a padded seat as the train ratcheted along its rusted rails. It took nearly half an hour to reach Zehlendorf. She exited and headed through the woods toward the Center.

Tracing a narrow wooded path, she passed the little lake where her mother used to bring her as a child. She remembered those baking summer afternoons, and how, during Muslim swim times, the lake was bursting with children, shrieking and splashing about. She remembered being 12 and swimming during Muslim time, when no men or boys were allowed near. She had wondered what boys her age were like when they swam. Aisha looked out across the lake, surrounded by a thicket of trees, moss and grass sloping down to the water. She saw herself propped up against the base of a gnarled oak, wrapped in a sodden towel, as Nilgul whispered in her ear that Germans swim naked. Aisha shook her head stubbornly. "You lie," she told Nilgul. "Not men and women together, total strangers." It was more the idea of being exposed to strangers than the nakedness that Aisha could not believe.

She shook herself back to the present. The lake was empty. There was no time for nostalgia. She approached the wellness center's glass doors and held her BIC to the scanner. Cameras scanned her retinas and fingerprints, matched them instantly with the card, and the glass doors slid silently apart. Mustafa would be glad to see her, Aisha thought, though she was never fully certain what lay behind his contented smile and glassy eyes.

Mustafa was only 16 when he was first admitted to the wellness cen-

ter at Schlachtensee. His alleged crime was stealing 200 grams of cheese from a local grocery store. But his behavior within the center made him a prime candidate for extended treatment. Today, six years later, Mustafa was a model patient. His productivity rates stood on a par with the best on his ward, and his supervisors often praised his agreeableness.

This wellness center had a proud history behind it, for it was one of the first of its kind to replace the old-fashioned prisons that had once littered Europe. Although a few antiquated prisons still remained in tiny, rural pockets of France and Spain, even these were scheduled to be phased out within a few years. But this wellness center in southwest Berlin was a model for rehabilitation institutes. Based on the groundbreaking work of psycho-biologist Horst Kettenacker, the Schlachtensee Center now housed over 1500 patients. Most politicians and policymakers agreed that the wellness centers had dramatically contributed to the sharp drop in street crimes across Europe.

Kettenacker, a member of the faculty of the University of Göttingen and former researcher at Pharmex, made his name with the publication in 2015 of his now seminal paper, "Life Chains of Desire." Kettenacker showed how every individual possesses an innate desire to complete the natural chains of human development: the desire to learn, the desire to form meaningful relationships, and above all the desire to work. In some individuals, however, the links in their natural life chains become severed or malformed. This is particularly true, Kettenacker demonstrated, for the chronically unemployed—those who refused to work for periods of three months or longer. This disruption in the natural human desire to labor most frequently manifests itself in the early stages of adulthood, especially for young men in their late teens and early twenties. These socially maladjusted individuals often distort their natural desire to labor into a desire for crime in a process, which Kettenacker termed "negative dislocation." But Kettenacker's most significant contribution was his discovery that through proper medication and a program of rigorous, continual labor, potential criminals could be transformed into obedient, productive members of society. They would, however, require extended, sometimes lifelong, residency within the nurturing, therapeutic confines of a wellness center. Kettenacker's research definitively showed the healing power of labor as a means of rejoining one's severed life chains.

Mustafa lived and worked in ward B, which specialized in textiles. While some wards collaborated with industry on developing plastics, paper products, or machine tools, others were devoted to assisting multinational corporations with data entry, customer service, or the handling of complaints. Patients at the centers typically worked between 12 and 14 hours per day. In exchange for their labor, the corporations that utilized their services covered the costs of a patient's medications, his room and board—an arrangement which most patients cheerfully accepted since their medications were prohibitively expensive. Although each patient's drug regimen was tailored to his particular needs, one of Kettenacker's most practical breakthroughs came in his discovery that a combination of Pacifix and Concentra dramatically improved patients' dispositions and enhanced their ability to focus. This minimum treatment helped patients to keep their productivity levels high while at the same time boosting their self-esteem.

There were, of course, certain unavoidable side effects from the treatment. Many patients contracted mild liver and kidney disorders, while others occasionally experienced paranoia and schizophrenia, but all of these conditions could be treated with additional medications at no extra cost to the patient. The long-term side effects were still not fully clear. While patients under treatment for ten years or longer showed higher than normal rates of brain damage, none of Pharmex's extensive studies had yet conclusively linked Kettenacker's treatment to this unfortunate result. Mortality rates had also been substantially reduced since the treatment's initial use. Today only 1 in 10,000 deaths were directly attributable to the treatment. Although the Pan-Islamic League and the Greens had fervently voted against most aspects of wellness center rehabilitation programs, it had to be admitted that violence within the centers was virtually unknown.

The story I have sketched above might sound fanciful, and indeed, it is merely a fictional account of one of Europe's possible futures. It is not, however, wholly implausible. One of Europe's distinguishing features since the late nineteenth century has been the rise of the welfare state. The growth of social democracy, a political movement that has sought to protect and nurture all members of society, has made parts of Europe an enviable place to live when one is in need of social services. It is less enviable if one resents paying 50 percent or more of one's income in taxes to support those services. As the number of Muslims increases across the continent, there is good reason to expect that the welfare state, as Europe has known it, will disintegrate, to be replaced by the privatization of services once thought solely the responsibility of the state. Here's why:

America may not even recognize Europe in a few short decades. Within the next ten to twenty years, as European society becomes more Muslim and more infused with those from non-European cultures, social democracy will break down. The welfare state that has characterized European governments, whether on the political Left or Right, since the Second World War, will begin to fracture under the stress of cultural heterogeneity.

In order for wealth redistribution to take root within a society, its citizens must possess a strong sense of shared identity. People will accept high taxation rates in exchange for generous social services so long as they believe that their wealth is being redistributed to others "like themselves." In other words, people can be persuaded to work in part for the benefit of others if they feel a common bond with the welfare recipients. Danes pay, for example, as high as 70 percent of their income in taxes. Italians, French, and Swedes all pay far higher taxes than do Americans. They have always done so, in part because they knew their money was going to other Danes, Italians, Frenchmen, or Swedes. They believed that they were giving a helping hand to those who shared their values, cultural norms, and work ethic.

This sense of social solidarity is certain to disintegrate as individual European states become more ethnically, racially, reli-

giously, and culturally diverse. Danes are already beginning to realize that their heavy tax burdens are going to support people who,
in their minds, are not Danes: they do not look the same, they
do not share their same religion, culture, or social norms. Most
critically, they have different values. At least, this is the perception that will grow over time, be it true or false. And when enough
Europeans come to resent working and sacrificing for those who
are seen as unlike themselves, they will resist income redistribution schemes. Social democracy will then die a painful death. It
will be painful, because it will mean a fundamental reordering of
European society. Europe will come to resemble America—only a
more extreme version.

One reason why social democracy never succeeded in the United
States is precisely because America is a starkly heterogeneous land.
Despite the melting-pot myth, Americans have rarely felt close
bonds with those of different races. One need only consider the
treatment of the Native Americans, African slaves, or Latino migratory farm workers. This does not mean that individual Americans have never overcome racial divides, but as a whole, American
society has demonstrated limited ability to forge deep interethnic
bonds—again, as Hurricane Katrina made abundantly clear.

Income redistribution can occur when the historical context
permits. In the ebullient 1990s, when it seemed that the Dow
and NASDAQ would rise forever, some economists triumphantly
declared that the great debate between Friedrich von Hayek and
John Maynard Keynes was over, and Hayek had won. They argued that Keynesian economics had led to deficit spending, infla-
tion, Leviathan bureaucracies, and growth-crushing welfare states.
Hayek, who prophesied a road to serfdom unless states adopted
liberalization and strict free-market principles, now appeared pre-
scient and vindicated by history—or so the argument ran.

The problem with such black-and-white debates is their failure
to consider the historical contexts. Each theory of political economy was necessitated by the spirit of the times. In postwar Europe,

laissez-faire was not a realistic option. The massive devastation of war necessitated government intervention, job programs to curtail widespread unemployment, and welfare programs to support the many who could no longer work and the many more who needed a helping hand as Europe recovered. Wealth redistribution was not only appropriate; the public demanded it.

But by the 1970s, Europe's economic recovery, fueled by the Marshall Plan and Germany's *Wirtschaftswunder* (economic miracle), were history, and the zeitgeist slowly began to shift. The Ronald Reagan and Margaret Thatcher economic revolutions called for curtailing redistribution and a cutting of taxes. The more affluent, successful members of society, they declared, should be able to keep more of what they earned. President Reagan spoke of welfare moms living in fancy hotels, cashing in their food stamps and welfare checks to live high on the hog—at the expense of hardworking families. Suddenly, the economically disadvantaged had become enemies of the state. Since then, the condition of single working mothers—black, white, Latina, and others—has grown steadily more tenuous. Taxation rates, however, have dropped substantially.

Bill Clinton and Tony Blair embraced and perpetuated the tenets that Reagan and Thatcher had popularized. Their political acumen is shown most clearly in their policies toward welfare. They sensed that the zeitgeist had shifted Right, and they had no intention of bucking the trend. Instead, they skillfully rode the tide of public opinion. In the early 2000s, even Germany's Social Democratic and Green coalition government bowed to that same public mood, lowering taxes and cutting social services. If these measures are shown to improve economic growth, the rest of Europe will likely follow the same course.

Neither Reagan and Thatcher nor Clinton and Blair forged a new consensus. They articulated a message that their publics were ready to hear. They did not lead; they followed. A Thatcherite running for office in 1946 Britain calling for cuts in social services in a war-ravaged land would have represented the lunatic fringe of society. She would have had no more success carrying that message in 1946 than an American politician calling for 70-percent taxation would have today. Wealth redistribution is contingent on the public's mood.

But what makes a society's mood change? Why do nations seem afflicted with bipolar disorder over time? It mainly comes down to cultural values. When people believe that their wealth is being given to those who share their values, they can be persuaded to bear heavy tax burdens. But if that perception changes, and people believe that they are working to support those with "foreign" values, resistance to redistribution will mount. Americans have grown increasingly resistant to taxation in part because of this belief. As Europeans come to believe the same about their Muslim neighbors, European socialism as we know it will end.

Muslims and other non-ethnic Europeans are just beginning to reach population levels high enough to concern ethnic Europeans. These "foreigners" with their perceived foreign values are becoming increasingly visible in major cities, from Paris and Berlin to Amsterdam and Madrid. Their share of news coverage is growing, with stories typically reporting on their incidence of crime, violence, or foreign practices such as wife-beating, honor killings, or female genital mutilation. Their objection to the publication of twelve Danish cartoons further reinforced the view that Muslim Europeans are opponents of free speech and the foundations of a democratic society. The public consciousness is rising, prejudices are being reinforced, and a public mood is slowly forming. This is what allows for the waxing popularity of right-wing, anti-immigrant, anti-foreigner political movements witnessed across Europe—even in countries like Holland, Denmark, and Switzerland, where tolerance and openness have long been their trademarks. Most of these far right-wing parties are unlikely to seize power, but they are likely to influence national and European-wide poli-

cies and to shape the public mood. Their impact will most strongly
be felt in the lowering of taxes, the cutting of social services, and
the gradual dismantling of the welfare state.

Extreme right-wing ideologues often exhibit a keen desire to
destroy the welfare state. Grover Norquist is arguably the most
influential man in America on the issue of tax reform. His impact
on the Republican Party cannot be overstated. Norquist, whom
the conservative television commentator Tucker Carlson once referred to as "a mean-spirited, humorless, dishonest little creep,"
has amassed countless influential supporters. He has spearheaded
a right-wing movement to slash taxes, stripping down govern-
ment-funded social services. He has even succeeded in persuading
222 U.S. congressmen and 46 senators to sign a pledge never to
raise taxes under any circumstances.[2]

At 49, Norquist, who is married to a Palestinian Muslim, has
headed Americans for Tax Reform, worked as a think-tank scholar,
and served as an economic advisor to the Bush administration.
Though single-minded in his drive to destroy welfare in America, he has also opined on the future of Europe's welfare state.
Norquist has argued that while it will not ultimately prevail over
America in a "battle of ideologies" for several reasons, Europe remains America's only true rival for global dominance. With its
promise of a welfare state, its sizeable population, a GDP comparable to America's, and a not inconsiderable military capability,
Europe, Norquist charged in 2003, possesses "a driving sense of
envy and anger at being surpassed by the barbarians of the New
World." Pointing to Europe's demographics and integration problems as prime factors in the continent's weakness, he urges the
United States to "relegate the European welfare state to the dust-
bin of history."[3] Actually, the United States may not need to lift a
finger in this endeavor: because of the values clash with its Muslim
minorities, Europeans may do the job themselves.

There are other ways in which Islam's influence across the continent may alter European identity. The fictional political party I created above, the Pan-Islamic League, will likely come to fruition, though probably under some other name. Religious groups have sometimes found their expression in organized political movements. The Catholic Center Party in Germany is one example, and of course the European-wide Christian Democratic Party has been a major force in postwar politics across the continent. A European-wide Muslim political party is a natural, and altogether hopeful, step toward greater integration. When it eventually emerges, it should be embraced, assuming its means and ends are peaceful and genuinely democratic.

If Muslim political participation rises, even if just at the national as opposed to the supranational level, relations with America could suffer. As Muslim Europeans wax in number and gain greater political enfranchisement, it is entirely likely that their impact on European foreign policy toward the Middle East, and toward the Muslim world more generally, will encourage a deeper division in transatlantic relations. We saw in chapter 2 some evidence of European and American divisions over the Israeli-Palestinian conflict. Europe's Muslims feel far stronger about their opposition to America's Israel policy than do ethnic Europeans. What Israel does to the Palestinians often triggers demonstrations and protests across Muslim Europe. We have seen in previous chapters how Israel and the United States are perceived by many Muslims as equivalent in their disregard for the value of Muslim lives. When the United States looks to its European allies for assistance in the Muslim world, especially if military measures are necessary, it could easily be rebuffed. America will then be forced to go it alone, the dangers of which, after Iraq, are now all too clear.

But these dire predictions need not come true, if we take wise actions today. In the final section, I outline some measures that Europe and the United States could adopt to ease the growing tensions across the continent. None but the most radical fundamentalists benefit from the state of layered ambivalence in which Muslim Europe now resides. The extremists profit because the larger the number of ambivalent second-circle Muslims, the greater are the extremists' odds of drawing some of them into their violent orbit. It is in everyone else's best interest to reduce the second circle's ambivalence, both to bolster social cohesion and to halt the breeding of future Bin Ladens.

Conclusion

LOOKING BACK
TO LOOK AHEAD

There is an old joke about what kind of future identity awaits the European Union. If all goes well, the joke goes, a European heaven will result, in which all the cooks will be French, the mechanics German, and the police British. Everyone will have an Italian lover, and the whole place will be organized by the Swiss. If things don't go as planned, the joke continues, a European hell will ensue, where all the cooks are British, the mechanics French, and Germans are the police. In EU hell, everyone's lover will be Swiss, and it will all be run by the Italians.

The joke was based on popular stereotypes of some of Europe's major peoples. If it were updated to reflect Europe's current composition, there would need to be some role for Muslims. Although the current tension over Islam's future in Europe leaves little room for humor, a new identity for Europe's Muslims will emerge. Guiding the development of that identity is the most serious challenge confronting Europe today, and it is an issue in which America has a clear and vested stake.

Why do the problems of Europe's Muslims matter? Three factors make the stakes especially high. The first is a question of security. The Madrid and London bombings, and the attacks on

American soldiers in Iraq committed by some of Europe's Muslims, make plain the urgent need to prevent Europe from becoming a breeding ground for future Bin Ladens.

The second factor surrounds the issue of European social cohesion. If a growing segment of the European population continues to feel alienated from mainstream society, social unrest will intensify.

The third reason involves the EU's still-forming identity. The face of Europe is rapidly changing. The mere presence of millions of Muslims, arriving as migrants and being born in greater numbers than their ethnic European counterparts, will unavoidably alter Europe's character. Europe might change peacefully into a multireligious, modern union, in which Muslims participate alongside non-Muslims in the democratic process. That would be a Europe in which mosques exist comfortably beside churches, where students wear headscarves or crosses of their own volition, and where wealth and opportunity are as accessible to Muslims as well as to non-Muslims. Or Europe could evolve into the dark scenario depicted in chapter 8: a continent on which Muslims feel excluded from the European identity, where they feel oppressed by state surveillance, religious profiling, or restrictions on their corporal freedom, and where increasing numbers are drawn to extremism.

Beyond these factors, there is an even greater reason why Europe's Muslims matter, not just to Europe or America, but to the whole world. How Muslim Europe evolves has repercussions for other regions around the globe. Here's why.

Europe is conducting an experiment, one never attempted before in human history. For much of the last two and a half millennia, Europeans have fought and died in a struggle for mastery over the continent. Caesars and Sun Kings, Napoleons and Habsburgs, Norsemen and Sultans, Nazis and Soviets, all have wrought death and devastation in a futile effort to rule Europe's fertile lands. Recognizing this senseless struggle's folly during the First World War, one man articulated a vision, and his concept slowly and steadily caught on. When Jean Monnet, a French international financier, helped lay the foundation for a European Community in 1950, he believed that a third continental war could only be avoided if the diverse European peoples pooled their sovereignty. Instead of seeing any one people rule the rest, Monnet envisioned a state of shared power in which Europeans would abandon some of their sovereignty to a democratically elected pan-European government. Out of this European Union a new identity would emerge.

Monnet's plan was a bold break with centuries of strife. If it succeeded and a new identity could be forged, he felt certain that Europe would be a bulwark of stability on the international stage. Yet, as farsighted as Monnet was, Muslims did not factor in his grand design.

Despite its periodic snags and setbacks, the EU has been steadily evolving for more than half a century. It has created a common currency, erected executive, legislative, and judicial institutions, trained and deployed its own military, and expanded to include twenty-five nations. And more countries hope to join, Turkey being primary among them. By seeking admission to the Union, nations are volunteering to abandon parts of their sovereignty. In return, they hope to gain membership in a peaceful, economically vibrant, politically stable supranational structure. The EU institutionalizes such a high degree of transnational interdependence that war among the member states seems hard to imagine. So far, the experiment appears to be working, serving as a model for other regions of the world. In 2002, an African Union formed, comprising all of Africa's 54 nations except Morocco. One day, an Asian economic union, modeled on the EU, might even arise. The hope is that the EU's success can be transplanted to other regions, bringing prosperity and peace to those countries as well. The free trade agreements of North America and Central America (NAFTA and CAFTA) exist in part as a response to the EU's success in eliminating trade barriers. Although a pan-American political union is unlikely to result, the knitting together of North and

South American economies, it is believed, can yield prosperity for all. These hopes have yet to be realized beyond Europe, and of course, in the longer view of human history, the EU is still at an embryonic stage. Nevertheless, its triumphs thus far are inspiring emulation around the world. For all these reasons, the new European identity cannot afford to fail. The stakes are too high, not just for Europe, but for the ripple effect its failure could have on the rest of the world.

If Muslims can be truly integrated into the European identity, to become fully at home in sharing Europe's most basic values of individual liberty, human rights, and democratic participation, then the great European experiment can succeed. At the same time, Muslim Europeans will inevitably change what it means to be European. It is conceivable that young, religious Muslims will push for greater social justice within the Union and greater international justice in Europe's foreign policies. Their influence could in time affect aspects of daily life as varied as the ways in which women's bodies are used to market consumer goods or the ways that banks do business. The only certainty is change. Ethnic Europeans, European Muslims, and Americans all must prepare for that change and attempt to direct its course.

The Values Question

This book's thesis is two-fold. First, Europe's failure to integrate its Muslims combined with America's battered image in the Muslim world have left too many Western Muslims easy prey for violent dogmas. Until America and Europe adopt new strategies, Europe will increasingly become the incubation ground for breeding Bin Ladens. Second, most younger European Muslims are not anti-American. They are better described as exhibiting ambivalent-Americanism, or *ambi-Americanism*. Beyond the many proximate causes of ambi-Americanism and ambi-Europeanism rests an underlying cause, a growing discomfort with mainstream European and American cultural values.

Why are Europe's Muslims caught in a state of layered ambivalence? If we can understand this, then many of the subsidiary questions can become clear, such as: Why is integration proving so difficult? Why are levels of Islamic fundamentalism rising? And why are some European Muslims turning to extremism?

Weak integration, rising fundamentalism, and increased extremism are all byproducts of ambi-Americanism and ambi-Europeanism. Grappling with the causes of ambivalence is a necessary step in resolving Europe's Muslim dilemma.

There are proximate causes for ambivalence. The first, of course, involves Muslims' perceptions of American and some European foreign policies. Diverse as they are, Europe's Muslims seem united in their opposition to the U.S.-led invasion and occupation of Iraq. But even before Iraq, many viewed American foreign policies as anti-Muslim. As Dilowar Khan, director of the East London Mosque, pointed out in chapter 1, there is considerable ill-will toward America among Muslims because of its policies toward the Muslim world, not just in Iraq. Global media like Al-Jazeera are continually bombarding Muslims with graphic images of Muslims embattled around the world, furthering a sense of siege and heightening a pan-Islamic identity.

Demographic pressures are furthering pan-Islamism. As Muslim birth rates remain high and ethnic European birthrates continue to fall, ethnic Europeans grow more fearful that their society is being overrun by "foreign" peoples, even if those peoples are European citizens as opposed to migratory laborers. As the public's fears grow, lawmakers and journalists focus more on Muslim differences and incidents of Muslim-related crime. All this fosters a vicious circle: the more numerous Muslims appear, the more attention is paid to their differences, and the more ethnic European fears are stoked. And as Islamophobia rises, Muslims gravitate toward identifying themselves as Muslims first. This scenario opens wide the doors to extreme fundamentalists, eager to exploit the susceptible young for their own perverted, violent ends.

These are the proximate causes of ambi-Americanism and ambi-Europeanism, but they are not the underlying cause. Before discussing that factor, I want to say a brief word about poverty. The voices I presented throughout this book come from European Muslims of different classes. Some have little: they are unemployed, underemployed, or struggling students. Others have much: doctors, psychologists, and professors. But nearly all felt varying degrees of ambivalence toward Europe and America. Many said they feel alienated from mainstream society. Poverty did not cause their ambivalence; other factors did.

Remember Mohammed Siddique Khan, the suspected leader of the July 2005 London bombings? He was the British citizen who videotaped a statement to the British public in English prior to his suicide attack on the London underground. The entire message lasted only two minutes and twenty-one seconds, some of that time being used by the Al Qaeda leader, Abu Musab al-Zarqawi. Given that Khan was about to give up his life for his beliefs and this was his sole opportunity to explain his actions to the world, it seems safe to assume that he thought carefully about his message and chose his words with care. Just before he explained his decision, he prefaced his remarks by saying: "Our driving motivation doesn't come from tangible commodities that this world has to offer."

Why would a man who is about to commit suicide and take the lives of many others with him use any of his precious few seconds of recorded explanation to mention tangible commodities? I think he chose these words with sober precision.

The roots of terrorism and the roots of ambivalence are not synonymous, but there is an overlap. The many causes of ambi-Americanism and ambi-Europeanism that Muslims express all have a core connection to values.

What inspired Khan to blow himself up was not solely his objection to British and American policies in the Middle East. His suicide bombing was instead the culminating act in a lengthy drama that began with his ambivalence toward British society. That ambivalence was ultimately based on his perception that the society did not share his Islamic values. One aspect of that view may have involved the conviction that British society was overly materialistic. But even if his reference to tangible commodities did not reflect a religious anti-materialist sensibility, the dissatisfaction with mainstream European values is reflected in the words and deeds of many others. This ambivalence may be more pronounced among European Muslims than it is among American Muslims because the former group are more economically disadvantaged than their American peers, but economic status cannot explain it all. Some American Muslims, such as Noor Saadeh, the woman who founded Razanne (the Muslim Barbie doll), are indicative of religious Muslims in America who share the ambivalence of their European counterparts.

Fortunately, the overwhelming majority of Europe's Muslims, and Muslims around the world, do not wish to blow themselves up or harm anyone else just because they feel ambivalent about mainstream European values. What they want instead is to change those perceived values to favor their interpretation of greater social justice—mainly for workers, women, migrants, and the poor. When they cannot change the mainstream society, they are separating themselves from it in small, but significant ways.

We can hear the distant echoes of Khan's frustration with consumerism in the clash of the Barbies I described in chapter 6. When the Muslim creators of Razanne, the Muslim Barbie, decided to make her modestly figured and dressed, and without the array of material possessions that Barbie owns, they were making a statement about mainstream consumer values. When the Islamic Bank of Britain declares in its slogan, "It's Your Choice," its founders are taking a religious stand against charging interest, something they see as an unethical business practice. When Zaid's explains that they are commanded to "pay their workers before their sweat dries," they are appealing to the Islamic value placed on economic justice, in contrast to an implied exploitation of workers by other companies. And when Qibla Cola and Mecca Cola donate a percentage of their profits to charity, they, too, are calling for social justice.

The primacy of these values for many European Muslims can be seen in Mahsa's life decisions. She is the British-born, Oxford-educated scientist profiled in chapter 2, who boycotted Marks and Spencer for its support of Israel. It can be seen in Velija, the drummer in a Hamburg band, who abstains from alcohol and being alone with young women. It's pronounced by Rafiq, the Saudi-born student in Prague, who feels men in Western societies go through women like cigarettes. It's being shouted from the burkas of Bengali women in the streets of London's Bethnal Green. It's stated from behind the veils of schoolgirls and schoolteachers who refuse to uncover, even when it means expulsion or unemployment. And it's reflected in the surveys that show a majority of younger Muslims affirming that one should not adapt too much to Western ways, but should instead live according to Islam.

The previous statement is perhaps the most concerning of all because it suggests that either the survey takers, or the survey makers, view Islam as incompatible with Western ways. That statement traverses through the heart of Europe's identity minefield. In fact, this is not the first time that Europe or America has confronted a religious minority that expressed deep ambivalence toward mainstream values. One historical example bears a striking parallel.

The Ultramontanes

To many Americans and Europeans, they seemed like religious fanatics. They often did not appear to be patriots. They observed peculiar forms of worship involving strange rituals. They procreated without restraint, producing unusually large families. In Massachusetts, many of their children refused to recite the Ten Commandments in school, as state law dictated. Mainstream scholars and pundits declared their beliefs antithetical to American ideas of freedom and democracy. They read their own separate newspapers about their co-religionists around the world, obsessing about injustices done to their people. They saw their co-religionists as brothers and sisters spread across foreign lands, and they threatened to remake the continent, and even the world, in accordance with their religious beliefs. This dangerous sect of religious extremists was known as Catholics, and their international political movement in the nineteenth century caused anxiety and outright fear among non-Catholics throughout much of the United States.[1]

Catholicism underwent a powerful revival in the nineteenth century under the banner of Ultramontanism. That term derives from the geographic perspective of most Europeans who saw the Pope as dwelling beyond the mountains (*ultra montanes*), those mountains being the Alps, separating Italy from the rest of Europe. Ultramontanism sought to spread a strict interpretation of Catholic teaching, with the Pope squarely at the Church's spiritual head. The movement opposed liberalism's emphasis on individual freedom, stressing instead the importance of community. It ardently defended the rights of workers and the poor. It objected to capitalism's perceived heartless indifference to the underclass. Its adherents called for greater social justice. In short, Ultramontanes were ardent social critics of mainstream American values, and they suffered from no shortage of Catholicophobia.

Searing anti-Catholicism emanated from the larger public. Even the more considered thinkers of the time tried to justify their prejudices with ill-conceived economic arguments. They pointed to the economic "backwardness" of Catholic countries and regions—Italy, France, Ireland, the Catholic cantons of Switzerland—compared to the relatively more prosperous Protestant nations—Britain, Germany, northern Ireland, and the Protestant Swiss cantons. In a similar way, Islamophobes today sometimes argue that the relative poverty of many Muslim countries is evidence of the religion's backwardness. (Ultramontanes were also castigated for their perceived support for authoritarianism, particularly Franco's Spain.)

Historical comparisons can never be perfectly analogous, but the situation of Europe's Muslims today with that of America's Catholics in the nineteenth century is worth considering. Some experts of current European affairs have compared Europe's Muslims to African Americans or Latino Americans of today. I think a comparison to Ultramontanes offers greater insight primarily because the underlying cause of both groups' ambivalence to mainstream society centers on values.

Consider some of the Ultramontane critiques of capitalism. A number of prominent Catholic thinkers in the middle and late nineteenth century voiced deep ambivalence about the unfettered free market. Matteo Liberatore, a leading Italian Jesuit, wrote: "Free competition is a terrible weapon, most effectual to crush the weak and reduce whole populations to economic slavery under a rod of iron wielded by the potent rulers of social wealth." Bishop Wilhelm von Ketteler of Mainz cautioned against an economic system that placed the worker's daily bread "at the complete mercy of the caprice of the market place." One French Catholic thinker criticized capitalism for its "speculation of usury." The popular newspaper *Catholic World* even asserted, "The theory of 'competition' as a solution of social and industrial disorder is as baseless as it is immoral."[2] As a result, these sentiments culminated in Pope Leo XIII's 1891 encyclical, *De Rerum Novarum*, which directly addressed capitalism and the question of workers' welfare. In the twentieth century, Ultramontanes also warned against the excesses of Hollywood films, the exploitation of women in the media, and above all the raising of the individual above the needs of a community.

Sound familiar? It should. Many of the Ultramontane concerns resemble those of European Muslims today. It was not surprising that both groups would speak out on questions of social justice. Catholics comprised a large portion of the urban, working class poor in nineteenth-century America. Similarly, European Muslims today are overrepresented in poverty and unemployment. Other values issues, such as those involving women, sexuality, or the plight of co-religionists worldwide, are comparable concerns of fundamentalist Christians in present-day America. The critical difference, of course, is that most American fundamentalist Christians consider themselves American. Even when they may feel ambivalent about mainstream practices (sex and violence on television, abortion, the death penalty, withholding life-support), they do not question their belonging to the nation. Europe's Muslims, conversely, are not yet sufficiently integrated. For too many, their identity as Europeans is in doubt.

When the Dutch Muslim Mohammed Bouyeri brutally murdered Theo van Gogh, or when the British Muslim Mohammed Siddique Khan blew himself up in the London underground, they were expressing the deepest form of anti-Americanism and anti-Europeanism. Fortunately, men like these remain on the radical fringe of Muslim Europe. Of even greater concern are the millions of European Muslims who reside within the second circle—drawn to many of America's and Europe's appealing traits, yet simultaneously repelled by their perceived un-Islamic values. Beneath their ambi-Americanism lies a religious core. They do not find some of their most basic values reflected in mainstream European and American culture. The values clash is the greatest challenge to a Muslim-inclusive European identity.

Europe's identity is changing, but Muslim Europe's identity is transforming as well. Whether out of the current values clash a new, inclusive European identity can be forged, or whether the value differences tear Europe's social cohesion asunder, remains to be seen. Although it took decades before the general public's fears of Ultramontanes receded, and the Catholics were not tainted by association with terror, perhaps the fate of the Ultramontanes can offer some hope. In time, the Ultramontanes pressed their agenda through democratic participation, and in the process wove themselves tighter into American society. As years passed, America's once feverish anti-Catholic sentiments subsided. For Europe's

Muslims to gain full citizenship rights and actively engage in the political process may be the best possible outcome to emerge from today's uncertain climate. If they come to feel fully integrated, fully accepted, as part of European society, their ambivalence will gradually fade away.

Although he did not have Muslims in mind at the time, Jean Monnet purportedly once said, "I always believed that Europe will be established through crises and not the sum of the outcome of those crises."[3] If managed wisely, and with a bit of luck, the clashes concerning Europe's Muslims might just propel Europe toward an ever closer union.

Epilogue

ATTRACTING
THE SECOND CIRCLE

On September 2, 2004, Republicans gathered in Manhattan, not far from Ground Zero at the World Trade Center site, to nominate George W. Bush as their candidate for president. A crowd of several thousand supporters enthusiastically cheered Governor George Pataki as he declared: "I thank God that on September 11th, we had a president who didn't wring his hands and wonder what America had done wrong to deserve this attack. I thank God we had a president who understood that America was attacked, not for what we had done wrong, but for what we do right."

Was America attacked because of what it does right? The tragic logic of Governor Pataki's statement means that if America continues doing what is "right," it should continue being attacked. Surely there must be a wiser approach to the problem of religious extremism. Tough talk sounds firm, but it will not solve the problem of terrorism. It will also preclude any hope of reaching out to the second circle, those Muslim millions who could either be drawn closer to mainstream American and European society, or pushed into the arms of extremists.

The scenario described in chapter 8 is undeniably grim, but that future is far from inevitable. Both Europe and the United

States can create a better future, despite the daunting difficulties integrating an ambivalent Muslim populace. The first step is to understand why so much ambivalence exists toward Europe and the United States. The next step is to devise policies that address the roots of ambivalence and work to create more favorable sentiments toward the West across Muslim Europe. But understanding has no chance to occur if our leaders have closed their minds.

William Bennett is one of the nation's leading conservative spokesmen on values. The former secretary of education under Ronald Reagan and the "Drug Czar" under George H. W. Bush, Bennett is now best known for his 88-week bestseller, *The Book of Virtues* (1993). Despite the revelations surrounding his serious gambling addiction, causing some to refer to this book as *The Bookie of Virtues*, he continues to opine on values-related issues. Speaking out on the causes of terrorism, he remarked: "Bad actions, wrong actions, even evil actions, have nothing to do with economics, poverty, wealth, or any other artificial construct any more than good actions do. They have to do with moral fiber. . . . Let's hear no more of root causes; let's speak, instead, of right and wrong and good and evil." Bennett's view, common among conservatives, says that brute force is the only answer. As he puts it: "I take bin Laden at his word: You show people a strong horse, and you show them a weak horse, and they will pick the strong horse every time—if they can still pick at all."[1]

The United States has demonstrated overwhelming force in Iraq, proving itself the strong horse. Yet many Iraqis sided with the weak horse, attacking U.S. soldiers on a daily basis. The Israelis have tried strong-horse tactics for decades, yet Palestinian resistance continued unabated, ending in the Israeli pull-out from southern Lebanon and later from Gaza. Bennett is wrong that people will pick the strong horse every time. He may be correct that poverty is not a sufficient root cause of terrorism, at least as far as Al Qaeda's leadership is concerned. But to ignore root causes is as foolhardy as to suggest that America is attacked because of what it does right. Neither perspective permits the United States to use its brains as well as its brawn in combating terror. For if there are no root causes, but simply bad people, then the United States must hunt down and kill every evil person intent on harming America. The problem, of course, is that every time one terrorist is killed, more emerge to take his place. It is not only wiser, but also infinitely more efficient, for the United States to give serious thought to why Muslims resent America. If they do, they can do more to prevent people from becoming terrorists in the first place.

Pataki's and Bennett's perspectives are not the sole domain of conservatives. In fact, they represent the mainstream thinking on the causes of ambi-Americanism within the Muslim world. These typically include the lack of freedom within Muslim states, poverty, evil individuals, and even Islam itself. Former Democratic congressman Lee Hamilton, vice chairman of the 9/11 Commission, crisply articulated the "lack of freedom" argument. Speaking of anti-American protests within Muslim states, he asserted, "There's a lot of dissatisfaction and anger with their own governments that are very repressive, and oftentimes, the leaders of these countries redirect the resentment and the hostilities that exist in the society, not towards their own governments, of course, but towards the United States."[2] From this vantage point, all forms of opposition—protest marches, economic boycotts, and destruction of property—can be rationalized as state-sponsored tactics, geared to divert domestic opposition.

Muslim Europe provides an excellent test for these assertions. No similar claims of government propaganda can be made of Europe's growing Muslim street. No state security services compel them to protest. No state-sponsored propaganda campaigns rail against the American lifestyle. Yet in the absence of state compulsion, Muslim Europeans have protested against American and European policies with which they disagree. They have launched boycotts of American and European consumer goods and their manufacturers. They have spawned competing products based on

Islamic values and pro-Muslim politics. They have voiced their anger at America across European-language websites. And they have taken to the polls when possible to register their opposition to perceived anti-Muslim policies. No, Muslim Europe's ambi-Americanism and ambi-Europeanism cannot be understood as a response to state censorship or state surveillance. Their discomfort with mainstream values springs from much more troubled waters: from Europe's failed integration policies, to America's battered image across the Muslim world, to homegrown Muslim extremists. If America and Europe are to attract the hearts and minds of second-circle Muslims, they dare not deny that real issues genuinely lie behind their ambivalence.

Spinning America

On January 18, 2005, Condoleezza Rice came before the Senate Foreign Relations Committee. At this day-long, intensive hearing, senators determined if she should be named the next U.S. Secretary of State. Senator Joseph Biden, the committee's ranking Democrat, approached Rice with a grave concern. Biden argued that it simply is not enough to invest in combating terrorism by military means alone. Instead, he explained, there are 1.3 billion Muslim hearts and minds that must be won, and the way to win them, he maintained, was through aggressive public diplomacy. "A major, major, major, major piece of our post-reconstruction effort in Germany and after World War II was diplomacy, public diplomacy," Biden explained. "We convinced many parts of the world that our ideas were ascendant, that we provided—we provided what is needed and would provide what was needed to bring security to the region and freedom. I remember when Lech Walesa first walked into my office like he did many of us here. He walked up, I said, 'Congratulations.' I said, 'Solidarity, ya, da, da.' He said, 'No, no, no, Radio Free Europe.'"[3]

Rice vowed that public diplomacy would be at the core of her State Department's mission. Her pledge and Senator Biden's concerns reflect the prevailing view among policymakers that America can attract moderate Muslims through its broadcasts, just as it did during the Cold War. Already on Valentine's Day 2004, President Bush gave an annual gift of $62 million to Muslims by launching Al-Hurra ("the free one"), America's first satellite TV station broadcast in Arabic and Farsi. The president declared that the station would counteract the "hateful propaganda that fills the airwaves in the Muslim world" and would tell "the truth about the values and the policies of the United States."[4]

To honor her pledge to beef up America's image abroad, Secretary Rice appointed, and Congress approved, Karen Hughes as undersecretary of state for public diplomacy. Formerly a White House communications director and a long-time close confidante of President Bush, Hughes is essentially America's chief spin doctor. She inherited an undeniably daunting task. As Patricia Harrison, assistant secretary of state for educational and cultural affairs, detailed America's public diplomacy efforts to the House International Relations Committee in August 2004, they aim to broadcast American values such as "rule of law, civil society, women's rights, religious tolerance and freedom of the media." Then she cogently added, "The vast majority of people around the world, including people in the Arab and Muslim world, share our values of freedom, human rights, opportunity and optimism, but many do not recognize America as champion of those values."[5] Harrison was absolutely right, but she neglected to say that many people around the world, particularly Muslims, also see the United States as championing certain other values that they reject, including a perceived disregard for social justice, an exploitation of women's bodies for commercial ends, and a pursuit of foreign policies intended to dominate world resources at the expense of others.

The president, Congress, and the State Department have begun investing millions of taxpayer dollars in broadcasts to win moderate Muslim hearts and minds. But their efforts are based on a one-size solution. They have fallen back on what worked during the Cold War and applied that historical lesson to the present. Unfortunately, these efforts will not succeed because moderate Muslims today exist under wholly different circumstances and harbor different desires than did Eastern Europeans in the Cold War.

Broadcasting American values of democracy, capitalism, and personal freedom did indeed help win the Cold War. Eastern Europeans, who waited hours in line for goods and decades for cars, often risked imprisonment by turning their antennas to the West to hear the hopeful *Voice of America*. Proponents of public diplomacy now advocate the same strategy in the war on terror. But this analogy is flawed. Those who felt trapped behind the Iron Curtain yearned for Western freedoms and opportunity. Today's Western Muslims already enjoy those freedoms, and many reject the West's perceived un-Islamic materialism. The surveys and interviews presented throughout this book show that young European Muslims, who are constantly exposed to American broadcasts of all sorts (CNN, films, TV shows), are deeply ambivalent toward many American values. If American broadcasts are not attracting European Muslims, they are unlikely to have much effect on Muslims in the Middle East, North Africa, or South Asia. Because the specific conditions of moderate Muslims today differ so fundamentally from those of East Europeans under communism during the Cold War, the government's one-size solution is almost certain to fail. Proponents of public diplomacy overlook its critical weakness in the war on terror. Successful use of public diplomacy depends not on how well American values are packaged and exported, but on whether American values are in fact attractive. Unfortunately, too many moderate Muslims around the world find too many mainstream American values repellent. To these people, no amount of clever packaging will make America more appealing.

Incensed at the persistent call for public diplomacy to bolster America's popularity in the Muslim world, one 20-year veteran of America's intelligence community has spoken out. "While important voices in the U.S. claim the intent of U.S. policy is misunderstood by Muslims, that Arabic satellite television channels deliberately distort the policy, and that better public diplomacy is the remedy, they are wrong. Bin Laden has been precise in telling America the reasons he is waging war on us. None of the reasons have anything to do with our freedom, liberty, and democracy but have everything to do with U.S. policies and actions in the Muslim world." [6] Those policies are often seen as a manifestation of America's values.

Orange Alert

In July 2004, security around the World Bank and International Monetary Fund increased dramatically as the terror alert level was raised to orange, the second-highest alert level, just below red. The threat was emanating from Al Qaeda. But why would Islamic extremists want to strike these international financial institutions?

Joseph Stiglitz, the Nobel Prize–winning economist and former vice president of the World Bank, explains in the introduction to his book, *Globalization and Its Discontents*, exactly why IMF policies have engendered so much resentment around the world. Rather than alleviating poverty, it has at times done much to further it. Stiglitz's entire book is a painful description of how the IMF and the U.S. Treasury have pursued policies that have not only favored the wealthy financial interests on Wall Street, but that have also made developing countries far poorer. Stiglitz concludes that after the IMF finds billions to aid the wealthiest within a nation and the foreign creditors, there is suddenly no money to be found for subsidies of food and fuel for the millions who have lost their jobs as a result of IMF policies. "No wonder," he says, "that there is so much anger against the IMF."

The IMF and World Bank are often seen as synonymous with the United States. They, like the United States, are viewed by many as not valuing social justice. As Stiglitz puts it: "The barbaric attacks of September 11th 2001 have brought home with great force that we all share the same planet. We are a global community, and like all communities have to follow some rules so that we can live together. These rules must be, and be seen to be, fair and just, must pay due attention to the poor as well as the powerful, must reflect a basic sense of decency and social justice."[7]

Stiglitz reminds us that in a globalizing world, what happens in remote regions of the earth can have consequences for Americans, especially if Americans are perceived as responsible for the plight of others. Many Muslims do not see the United States as a society that values social justice, especially as America's own rich-poor gap widens. In America, 97 percent of the increase in wealth over the last twenty years has gone to the top 20 percent of families, while the bottom 20 percent watched its earnings drop by 44 percent. Forty percent of the country's wealth is owned by 1 percent of the population, while 12.5 percent live in poverty.[8] The number of people living in poverty in America has risen for four consecutive years. In the first three years following President Bush's tax cuts, the number of people living in poverty rose by 3.5 million, but the income of the four hundred wealthiest Americans rose by 10 percent in 2002 alone.[9] Policymakers must realize that if their actions are seen to perpetuate poverty or injustice, they will drive away second-circle Muslims.

The Religious Right Weighs In

Attracting hearts and minds is made more difficult when our religious, as well as our political, leaders help to repel second-circle Muslims from America while simultaneously spreading misinformation about Islam.

Was Mohammed a terrorist? Probably the best-known Christian leader in America (after Billy Graham, who is an international icon) is the Reverend Jerry Falwell. Falwell has been stridently critical of Islam, even to the point of calling Islam's founder, Mohammed, a terrorist. In an episode of the weekly CBS news magazine show, *60 Minutes*, Falwell said: "Muhammad was a terrorist. I read enough of the history of his life written by both Muslims and non-Muslims [to know] that he was a violent man, a man of war. In my opinion . . . Jesus set the example for love, as did Moses. And I think that Muhammad set an opposite example." The preacher later appended his remarks by insisting, "I've said often and many places that most Muslims are people of peace and want peace and tranquility for their families and abhor terrorism. Islam, like most faiths, has a fringe of radicals who carry on bloodshed wherever they are."[10] But watching a nationally televised Falwell sermon on Islam is an extraordinary event. The preacher disparages Mohammed for a variety of acts, including his taking of eleven wives, the youngest, Aisha, being only nine. Falwell stopped short of labeling Mohammed a polygamous pedophile, but the implications were clear. Falwell has also charged that "pagans, abortionists, feminists, homosexuals and civil liberties groups had secularized the nation and helped the September 11th attacks happen," a remark for which he later apologized.

These episodes of religious name-calling are not hermetically sealed discourses confined to America. In a globalizing world, inflammatory comments reverberate overseas. Falwell's comments splashed across the front pages of Pakistani newspapers, and shortly thereafter the extreme Islamist parties won fifty seats in parliamentary elections, a startling result compared to their usual four seats. Across India, riots between Hindus and Muslims erupted in several towns after Falwell's anti-Muslim comments were aired on Indian television. In the mostly Muslim state of Jammu-Kashmir, thousands demonstrated against America and threw rocks. In the city of Solapur, in Maharastra state, at least ten people were killed and more than 140 injured in riots allegedly spawned by Falwell's remarks. Iranian cleric Mohsen Mojtahed Shabestari, a representative of Iran's Supreme Leader Ayatollah Ali Khamenei, issued a fatwa, saying that Falwell was a mercenary and must be killed. And when IslamOnline discussed the Falwell controversy, it linked Falwell to Israel. The Rev. Jerry Falwell has a long history of advocating hatred and intolerance. Interestingly, he is also one of the most vocal (or rather leading) supporters of the state of Israel in America today. Considering this, his anti-Muslim rant in a 2001 interview with Belief.net is not the least bit surprising.[11]

Pat Robertson is another of America's best-recognized Christian leaders. Robertson has never shied from politics. In fact, he even made a run for president in 1984. In August 2005, Robertson called for the assassination of Venezuelan President Hugo Chàvez, compelling the Bush administration to declare that the preacher's remarks did not reflect any American policy. It was not the first time Robertson had used inflammatory words. In October 2001, Robertson said on his nationally syndicated, Christian-oriented, 700 Club program, "If you get right down to it, Osama bin Laden is probably truer to Mohammed than some of the others." Quoting from the Quran, Robertson argued that Islam advocates fighting and killing infidels, making Islam a war-like doctrine. Robertson did not point out similar calls for murder in the Old Testament. He did, however, add that Western leaders would benefit from reading the Quran in the same way that earlier Western leaders should have read Hitler's *Mein Kampf*. Robertson, too, is an ardent supporter of Israel.

America's religious right is not solely Christian. Rabbi Dennis Praeger, a long-time Los Angeles radio talk show host and frequent commentator on international affairs, recently contributed to a collection of essays on America's role as a superpower. To gain a sense of how Praeger sees the divisions between Europe and the United States, consider first his opinion of American foreign policy: "America is a light in this dark world. . . . No other country approaches America as a force for good on planet Earth. If a meteor destroyed the United States at this time, the world would be overrun by cruelty. The world needs a policeman, just as individual countries need policemen and humanity should thank God every day that it is the United States of America that has the power and the moral will to be the world's policeman and not France, or China, or Russia or any other country."[12]

Praeger's views stand in sharp contrast to the way most Muslims, certainly Europe's Muslims, perceive American foreign policies. Turning to the Middle East, Praeger spells out frankly what may be a commonly held view in America. One of the differences between the New and Old Worlds, Praeger believes, is the opposing interpretation of which side is to blame for ongoing conflict. "America believes that little Israel needs to be supported in its battle for survival against those who wish to annihilate the Jewish state. Europe believes that America and Israel are the problem, not Hamas, Islamic Jihad, and the Islamists."[13]

Praeger puts his finger on a key difference between Americans and Europeans. According to a survey conducted in fifteen EU member states, an average of 60 percent of respondents ranked Israel as the greatest threat to world peace, followed by Iran, North Korea, and then the United States. The only exception was the Greeks, 88 percent of whom ranked the United States as the greatest threat. When this poll's findings were released in November 2003, European leaders rushed to distance themselves from the survey, charging the study as anti-Semitic. However, in a May 2003 survey of world opinions by the Pew Research Center, pluralities or majorities in twenty out of twenty-one populations declared that they believe the United States favors Israel over the Palestinians too greatly. Americans are the only exception: Even Israelis believe America favors Israel too much, with 47 percent holding this view, while 38 percent say its policy is fair and 11 percent think the United States favors the Palestinians too much.

These divergent views between Americans and Europeans over the Middle East have potent implications for Europe's Muslim dilemma. Many of Europe's Muslims share their host nation's anti-American sentiments, particularly over the sensitive Palestinian issue, but Europe's Muslims often feel a far deeper sense of outrage toward both Israel and the United States.

How deep the transatlantic divide becomes will in large part be driven by Europe's changing face. The demographic pressures, from Muslim birthrates to immigration, are reshaping the continent's ethnic and religious composition. Rabbi Praeger takes a somewhat apocalyptic view of these patterns: "Americans reproduce and take in immigrants, many of whom share their views. Europeans do not reproduce—the purpose of life for most secular Europeans is to have fun and children are a real pain. . . . Europe will either have a civil war with its immigrants, most of whom loath the West, or it will peacefully become Muslim. America will survive and thrive as the Judeo-Christian society it has always been unless the Americans who wish to destroy that identity prevail."[14] The situation may not be quite as stark as Praeger predicts, but bridging the gap between Americans, ethnic Europeans, and Europe's Muslims will not be easy. It will require far more than simply spin.

New Approaches

America and Europe need new approaches in the effort to attract Muslim hearts and minds. Hard power is still the only effective means for combating diehard terrorists. Soft power is essential for winning the support of allies already inclined to their side. But the bulk of people America needs to win over are neither terrorists nor allies. They are moderate, religious Muslims, disenchanted with many mainstream American and European values and deeply ambivalent about their policies.

This epilogue outlines some modest measures, and a few bolder ones, for reaching out to the millions of ambivalent Muslims within Europe's second circle. But before any such efforts can begin, we need to change the way we speak about the problem.

End the War of Ideas

America and Europe should stop using metaphors of war such as the "war of ideas" and the "battle for hearts and minds," especially in official statements.[15] By casting the issue in terms of a conflict, America repels the very people it hopes to attract. The war metaphor frames Muslims either as enemies with ideas to be conquered, or as territory on a battlefield to be occupied and controlled. That kind of language automatically forces people into one camp or another. Those Muslims who already have negative associations with American wars will be further repelled. If a metaphor must be used in the approach to second-circle Muslims (a phrase that is itself relatively neutral), then employing metaphors of attraction and justice is wisest.

You might be thinking, "Isn't this just another type of spin doctoring, the very thing just criticized?" The difference is this: Language should be accurate. Unless the European and American governments actually perceive Muslims as enemies, or as inhabiting ideological territory to be conquered, the war metaphor is misleading, not to mention counterproductive. If people are already ambivalent, then by forcing them to take sides in a with-us-or-against-us ultimatum, America makes itself less attractive. Spin doctoring, on the other hand, is an attempt to convince people of something untrue, or a stretch from the truth. Public diplomacy campaigns that try to persuade Muslims that America supports individual freedoms, private enterprise, or technological development reflect truths already known to most Muslims and therefore hold little value. Campaigns that seek to persuade Muslims that America was acting solely in Muslims' best interests by invading and occupying Iraq are not believable, and therefore make the United States appear untrustworthy. If such an assertion is true, Muslims ask, why would so little care have been taken to protect the Iraqi populace after the war, why was the infrastructure not better defended, why were cluster bombs used that killed and maimed children, and so on. These are legitimate questions that Muslims (and others) pose. If they are confronted head-on and answered sincerely, then public diplomacy can be effective. If, instead, the government tries to put a positive spin on such issues, public diplomacy will surely fail.

Modest Proposals

Below are some minor, micro-programs that could help begin to attract Europe's second-circle Muslims by aiding their integration into European society. Their purpose is not primarily to reduce poverty, though this in itself would be worthwhile. They are intended foremost to foster integration. They cannot substitute for macro-policies, but they can serve as immediate and highly actionable measures for policymakers. I offer some broader policy suggestions in the subsequent section.

Europe's Muslims Need a Head Start

America possesses a powerful secret weapon in the war on terror—one so secret that its creators haven't yet realized it exists. But if Europe could obtain the weapon's blueprints, it could combat the roots of terror, integrate its Muslim residents, and bolster transatlantic relations in a single strike. Best of all, deploying this weapon will represent a naked act of preemption that the global community can respect and admire.

Launched in the United States in 1964, the Head Start program sought to provide early education for children of low-income families. Though targeted at the poorest classes, the program actually assisted many ethnic and racial minorities, as the problems of class and race are commonly intertwined. Head Start hoped to head off the social problems that often result from disproportionate minority school drop-out rates: higher unemployment, social alienation, petty and sometimes violent crime. Since its founding, the program has been a notable success. More than 20 million children have graduated from its courses, acquiring social and academic skills. Although critics have charged that Head Start's graduates have not performed as well as their more affluent peers, defenders note that the children have fared far better than their underprivileged counterparts who never experienced the program at all. Head Start has not remedied all the inequities of class and race, but it has had a positive impact on many of its participants and the society in which they live. If adapted to European needs, Head Start could play a critical role in uplifting Europe's Muslim underclass.

Europe's integration problem begins at an early age. Since many immigrants hail from the poorer, less literate regions of North Africa, South Asia, Eastern Turkey, and the Middle East, and like most immigrants, tend to settle within geographically close communities, the children are raised in homes where distinctive dialects are spoken, parents are unable to read to their children in the host country's language, and less contact with ethnic Europeans is available. For example, a typical Berlin preschool class in a heavily Muslim area can contain mostly Turkish pupils. Consequently, the Turkish children speak mainly among themselves, and they enter the school system with insufficient German language skills. In other words, Europe's Muslims begin the education marathon already behind the pack.

The combination of increased viewership of Turkish and Arabic channels on satellite television and Muslim mothers who lack German language skills means that a new generation of Muslim children receive limited exposure to European languages and culture. In previous decades, immigrants had little choice but to learn the host nation's language, but with the proliferation of modern global media, access to satellite TV and the Internet make it possible to remain more closely connected to foreign events, all in the mother tongue. Without an early immersion in the host country's language and customs, Muslim children are more likely to leave school too soon, struggle finding work, and drift down the slippery slope of social alienation, and may in some instances turn to violence.

To avert this, Europe might enlist the aid of American Head Start administrators and teachers to establish Head Start for Muslim preschoolers, adapting the program to fit local needs. The American Head Start program targets preschoolers aged 0–5.

Classes may be held in local community centers and can cover a wide range of subjects, from language to nutrition to social etiquette and customs. In the past, specialized adult literacy programs for foreign-born workers were created in Berlin and other German cities. When it was discovered that Muslim mothers were only willing to attend such programs if their young children were with them rather than left in daycare centers, organizers made the necessary adjustments and experienced far greater attendance. Wherever the classes are held, the program may have greater success if Muslim mothers are permitted to attend.

Head Start teachers could be drawn from the Muslim community, particularly women possessing fluency in the host country's language along with a strong knowledge of European customs. Employing Muslim women would give these individuals a greater stake in European society and reduce their sense of alienation. Teachers could be assisted by the many student teachers seeking placements for their practicums, and in Germany by young men serving their *Civildienst*. This would enable young ethnic Europeans to interact closely with Muslims, creating greater familiarity with a culture that too often seems foreign and opaque.

Of course, the program would require state funding at a time when many European economies remain flat. However, by drawing on labor from *Civildienst* men and student teachers, the labor costs of employing professional daycare workers could be reduced. If, at the outset, the program could resist the temptation to establish a cumbersome bureaucracy, administrative expenses could potentially be modest. Whatever the costs, if a European Head Start succeeds, the investments today will be far less than the costs of social fragmentation and unrest which could plague the continent in the future.

By providing intensive early language, culture, and basic preschool education, many of the later difficulties Muslim children experience in school can be reduced. This is a long-term strategy that can have a palpable impact on integration fifteen to twenty years from now, just as the demographic pressures from rising Muslim birthrates will be imposing their greatest strains on European society. There are no guarantees that better integration will necessarily prevent terrorism. But the experience of other countries, including the United States, suggests that alienated minorities with little or no access to political power, and who feel socially and economically disadvantaged, often produce a fringe element that turns to violence. If Europe is to win the race against domestic fragmentation from a demographic danger, it must give its Muslim children a generous head start.

Targeted Microlending

In 1995, the EU embarked on an admittedly ambitious project: the creation of a European-Mediterranean Partnership. The EMP, commonly known as the Barcelona Process, encompassed the then fifteen EU member states along with Algeria, Cyprus, Egypt, Israel, Jordan, Lebanon, Malta, Morocco, Syria, Tunisia, Turkey, and the Palestinian Authority. The aim was to create a free-trade zone comprising the region's 700 million inhabitants, spur economic development and civil society in Muslim lands, and in turn reduce the threat of Islamic extremism to the extent that its roots stem from the north-south, rich/poor gap. In the decade since its inception, the Barcelona Process has gone nowhere. As one observer put it: "The EU says, 'Take this money, the norms, and the practices, go create your own region and, thus, give us your stability.' To the South, however, the Barcelona Process has so far meant, at best, euros, and, at worst, a neocolonialist plot."[16]

Rather than transferring euros to spur development in regions where liberal capitalism and democracy are limited, the EU would meet with greater success by investing euros directly into Europe's Muslims. Microlending has a proven track record of poverty reduction. It has been so successful that in 2003, Deutsche Bank announced plans to open a $50 million fund to invest in microfinancing organizations. Banks are coming to see microfinancing not as charity, but as smart business sense. Stanley Fischer, former deputy director of the International Monetary Fund and current Citigroup vice chairman, has noted that when the 1997 East Asian financial crisis struck, one Indonesian bank suffered a near 100 percent default rate from its corporate portfolio, but only a 2 percent default rate from its microlending portfolio. EU states and the United States should combine with major banking institutions to extend targeted microloans to enable Europe's Muslims to start or grow small businesses; this step would help make Muslims greater stakeholders in European society, uplift their socioeconomic standing, and mitigate their sense of alienation. At the same time it would provide a fillip to European economic growth and probably do more to facilitate Mediterranean economic development as a result of increased remittances from Europe's Muslims to their families back home.

Send Young Americans to Muslim Countries

Since the 9/11 Commission published its recommendations, both the U.S. Congress and the State Department have been speaking more about increasing student visa programs. The stated aim is to expose young Muslims to the openness of American society so that they will return with a better image of our country. The thrust of this book has been to suggest that it is even more important for Americans to understand the Muslim perspective. Therefore, more funding should go toward sending young Americans to study in Muslim states. Just as Senator William Fulbright gave his name to a study-abroad program, today a new, well-funded program is needed to send significant portions of American students to the diverse Muslim world, either under Fulbright auspices or through specialized scholarship. If more Americans possessed a deeper understanding of the religious Muslim perspective by having lived in Muslim states, they should be more likely to support national policies that promote American interests without repelling religious Muslims.

Broader Measures

Assessing America's vulnerabilities, the 9/11 Commission concluded, "Before 9/11, the United States tried to solve the Al Qaeda problem with the same government institutions and capabilities it had used in the last stages of the Cold War and its immediate aftermath. These capabilities were insufficient, but little was done to expand or reform them." The same can still be said about the American government's attempts to attract the second circle. The Bush administration has brought about the largest reordering of American government since the New Deal, spending billions of dollars on creating a Department of Homeland Security and the post of National Intelligence Director. All of these efforts have been targeted at stopping hardened terrorists, a group that could be as small as 50,000 people worldwide. Except for some talk about improving public diplomacy, no meaningful reorganization has occurred to address second-circle Muslims and prevent them from entering the extremists' camp. The U.S. government needs to be as devoted to attracting second-circle Muslims as it is to thwarting violent fanatics.

What follows are a few broad changes at the federal level that could help focus greater attention on the second circle. These are not policy prescriptions themselves. Specific policies would need to address issues such as the problem of torture, secret prisons, or the denial of basic human rights to terror suspects. These issues have so dramatically undermined America's appeal within the second circle that broader measures are required merely to undo the damage wrought from Abu Ghraib to Guantánamo. As former President Jimmy Carter put it, "Torture demonstrates weakness, not strength. It does not show understanding, power, or magnanimity. It is not leadership. It is a reaction of government officials overwhelmed by fear who succumb to conduct unworthy of them and of the citizens of the United States."[17] Carter notes that U.S.

intelligence officials estimated that 70 to 90 of those held at Abu Ghraib were held by mistake, and that military officials have reported that since 2002, at least 108 prisoners have died in American custody in Iraq, Afghanistan, and other secret locations, with homicide as the cause of death in 28 cases. As policies such as extraordinary rendition become increasingly well known, America drives away the second circle Muslims it needs to attract.

Rather than outlining particular policies, I have sketched below some measures that could help policymakers think differently, and more effectively, about the problem of ambi-Americanism and ambi-Europeanism. All are relatively inexpensive, especially when compared to the money already spent on combating the much smaller inner circle of terrorists.

Creating Intentional Interdependence

Despite the obvious differences between a guerrilla campaign in Vietnam and a global war on terror, there may well be lessons to be drawn from America's defeat in Vietnam. The North Vietnamese proved superior in gaining popular support from those who could have been drawn into the American camp. One highly effective tactic they employed involved a process of "intentional interdependence." Unlike the South Vietnamese Army (ARVN), which was entirely dependent on the Americans for financial and military backing, the Northern Liberation Front (NLF) made itself dependent on local Vietnamese. The villagers understood that the ARVN was beholden to the Americans, not to the villagers. The ARVN had no incentive to respond to their needs, or even to treat the villagers with decency. In sharp contrast, NLF cadres made themselves dependent on the food, housing, and aid of Vietnamese villagers. The villagers then recognized that the North Vietnamese would be sensitive to their needs because those fighters needed their support. In other words, creating intentional interdependence helped the North to win the battle for hearts and minds.

On September 12, 2001, America missed a golden opportunity. Countries around the world offered their assistance, each with specialized rescue squads. If Washington had accepted these generous offers of assistance, particularly from Muslim states, it would have done much to redress its massive aid imbalance. Following Hurricane Katrina, the United States did accept international aid, including that from Muslim states. Accepting financial aid was a small first step toward interdependence. America needs to find areas where it genuinely needs the help of Muslims. The first, most obvious area, is to need their aid in devising strategies for the hearts-and-minds campaign.

America already has a close ally with particular expertise in attracting Muslim hearts and minds. Turkish Prime Minister Erdogan leads a reformed Islamist party that came to power on a popular mandate. Part of his party's success resulted from years of on-the-ground, regular close contact with rural Turks and from redistributing wealth to those who needed it most. Even if these tactics are not appropriate for America, the U.S. government should be as open to learning from other countries and adapting their methods. America should be as active in seeking its allies' aid in the hearts and minds campaign as it is in the military, financial, and intelligence aspects of the war on terror.

Council of Historical Advisors

The U.S. government should create an inexpensive, permanent, and independent body to advise the president on matters of policy perception. Modeled on the three-member Council of Economic Advisors, the Council of Historical Advisors would consist of three accomplished, senior historians or regional area experts drawn from academia. These three individuals, serving for one- or two-year appointments and supported by a small staff of research assistants, would provide the president with independent, nonpartisan advice on how the historical context within a country or a region is likely to impact American policies. Many scholars believe that the

United States suffered such a devastating defeat in Vietnam partly because it failed to understand the country and the people it was trying to assist. America's struggles in Iraq may have been likewise impaired. The Council would offer more in-depth, independent advice than State Department bureaucrats or National Security Council political appointees are capable of providing. Advisors such as these are hamstrung by the system in which they function, for their careers often hinge upon their willingness to support the president's favored approach.

Drawing on academia to assist policymakers is not unprecedented. In the summer of 1941, President Roosevelt encouraged the formation of a small body of scholars and military officers to assess foreign intelligence. Among the founding members of the Office of the Coordinator of Information was Harvard historian William L. Langer. Although other governmental agencies, fearing a diminution of their authority, initially resisted cooperating with this new body, the attack on Pearl Harbor brought home the critical need for greater intelligence analysis. The OCI was later renamed the Office of Strategic Services, which in 1947 became the Central Intelligence Agency. Prof. Langer, an expert on European diplomatic history, served as head of the Research and Analysis Branch, a precursor of today's National Intelligence Council, which attracted other historians and scholars with regional expertise. Once World War II ended, Langer's bureau assembled Russia scholars, who prepared the first national intelligence estimate on the Soviet Union.[18]

If 9/11 was the Pearl Harbor of today's global war on terror, then a new body of scholars should be enlisted to aid policymakers—this time not for intelligence assessments, but rather to enhance policy effectiveness. Whereas the U.S. government once demanded the greatest number of area experts on Germany, Japan, and later the Soviet Union, today's need is for scholars of the Muslim world. While academics are sometimes asked to serve in already-existing policymaking posts (always as political appointees), the president currently lacks an independent body of advisors. Under skilled direction, the Council could vastly improve American foreign policy toward the Muslim world, and toward other regions as well.

Second-Circle Contact Group

The U.S. government often establishes multinational coordinating councils to facilitate specific objectives in which multiple countries hold high stakes. Recent examples include the Core Group, responsible for coordinating tsunami relief efforts, and the contact group established to foster Balkan peacekeeping measures. Because the United States and EU have significant, overlapping interests in attracting second-circle Muslims, America should urge the creation of a second-circle contact group.

Spain is pursuing a cross-cultural dialogue to defuse interfaith tensions. France is pushing a "Marshall Plan" for Muslim ghettos to lift Muslims out of poverty and avert new riots. Britain has launched a hearts-and-minds campaign for training moderate imams. Despite the common problems facing Western Europe, no coordinated strategy yet exists at the EU level. Because America also has a clear security stake in the fate of Western Muslims, relevant officials and scholars (Muslim and secular) from the United States and EU nations with significant Muslim populations (Germany, France, Britain, and Holland) should meet regularly to explore the linkages between disaffected Western Muslim populations and global/domestic terrorism. This body should examine Muslim identity and integration issues in democratic societies and provide recommendations for engaging Western Muslims. By comparing the experiences of various democratic governments with second-circle Muslims, the contact group should be able to offer practical solutions to address common threats, no matter the form, be it domestic unrest, crime, or extremism. By sharing solutions to common problems and by coordinating integration efforts, the United States and EU will more effectively attract second-circle Muslims and reduce the risk of Islamic extremism. By investing energy and resources into integration strategies, America can send a clear and powerful message to Western Muslims, and to the broader Muslim world, that America is not the enemy of Islam, but instead values justice, one of Islam's highest virtues.

Appendix

Islamic Population by Country—Europe and United States

Country	Population (2005E)	% Muslim	Muslim Total
Albania‡	3,563,112	70	2,494,178
Andorra‡	70,549	n/a	n/a
Austria	8,184,691	4.7	384,680
Belarus‡	10,300,483	0.5	51,502
Belgium	10,364,388	3.5	362,753
Bosnia and Herzegovina‡	4,025,476	40	1,610,190
Bulgaria†	7,450,349	12.2	908,942
Croatia†	4,495,904	1.3	58,446
Cyprus	780,133	18	140,423
Czech Republic	10,241,138	0.2	20,482
Denmark	5,432,335	3	162,970
Estonia	1,332,893	n/a	n/a
Finland	5,223,442	0.2	10,446
France	60,656,178	7.5	4,549,213
Germany	82,431,390	3.7	3,049,961
Greece	10,668,354	1.3	c300,000
Hungary	10,006,835	0.6	60,041
Iceland‡	296,737	0.1	321
Ireland	4,015,676	0.49	19,676
Italy	58,103,033	1.7	987,751
Latvia	2,290,237	0.02	458

Country	Population (2005E)	% Muslim	Muslim Total
Liechtenstein‡	33,863	2.4	1,384
Lithuania	3,596,617	0.6	21,579
Luxembourg	468,571	2	9,371
FYR Macedonia‡	2,045,262	30	613,578
Malta	400,000	1.3	ca 3,000
Moldova‡	4,455,421	0.07	3,118
Monaco‡	32,120	n/a	n/a
The Netherlands	16,407,491	6	984,449
Norway‡	4,593,041	1.6	73,488
Poland	38,635,144	0.008	3,090
Portugal	10,566,212	0.35	36,981
Romania†	22,329,977	0.3	66,989
Russia‡	143,420,309	15	21,513,046
San Marino‡	28,100	n/a	n/a
Serbia-Montenegro‡	10,829,175	21	2,274,126
Slovakia	5,431,363	0.05	2,715
Slovenia	2,011,070	2.5	50,276
Spain	40,341,462	2.5	1,008,536
Sweden	9,001,774	4	360,070
Switzerland‡	7,489,370	4.4	329,532
Turkey†	69,660,559	99	68,963,953
Ukraine‡	47,425,336	0.5	237,126
United Kingdom	60,441,457	2.7	1,631,919
United States	295,734,134	1.4	4,140,277

Source: The percentage of Muslim population of each country was taken from the U.S. State Department's *International Religious Freedom Report 2004* (www .state.gov/g/drl/rls/irf/). Other sources used were CIA *World Factbook* (www.cia.gov/ cia/publications/factbook/) and adherents.com (www.adherents.com/Na/Na_321 .html#2058). In a few cases of conflicting estimates, the average of the lowest and highest estimates was calculated. The total population of each country was taken from U.S. Census Bureau 2005 estimates (www.census.gov/cgi-bin/ipc/idbrank.pl).

　† Applicant for EU membership in 2007

　‡ Not a member of the EU

Notes

Introduction. The Prolific Assassin

1. Richard Clarke, "What We Owe Iraq," *Washington Post*, Nov. 21, 2004.

2. Pamela Hess, "Arab Opinions of U.S. Very Negative," UPI, Dec. 7, 2005, at www.zogby.com.

3. Pew Global Attitudes Project 2005, June 23, 2005, www.pewglobal .org/reports. See also Pew Global Attitudes Project 2004, "A Year after Iraq War," Mar. 16, 2004, www.people-press.org/reports.

4. Wilhelm Heitmeyer, Joachim Muller, and Helmut Schroeder, *Verlockender Fundamentalismus: Turkische Jugendliche in Deutschland* (Frankfurt a.M.: Suhrkamp, 1997).

Chapter 1. London Bridges

1. Pew Global Attitudes Project 2005, June 23, 2005, www.pewglobal .org/reports.

2. Alan Cowell, "Al-Jazeera Video Links London Bombing to Al-Qaeda," *New York Times*, Sept. 2, 2005.

3. Hassan M. Fattah, "Anger Burns on the Fringe of Britain's Muslims," *New York Times*, July 16, 2005.

4. Peter Bergen and Paul Cruickshank, "The Dangers of Tolerance," *New Republic*, Aug. 8, 2005.

5. At the time of this writing, the East London mosque is licensed to operate its radio station only during the month of Ramadan.

6. I am being especially vague on certain details of Faisal's life in order to safeguard his identity.

7. Muslim Council of Britain Open Letter to Imams, Mar. 31, 2004, www.mcb.org.uk.

8. Inayat Bunglawala, "We Must Unite to Defeat This Threat," *Daily Express*, Apr. 26, 2004.

9. MCB Press Release, Aug. 5, 2005.

10. MCB Press Release, Mar. 22, 2004.

11. MCB Press Release, Apr. 8, 2004.

Chapter 2. Islamic Awakenings

1. Foreign and Commonwealth Office, "Advice to British Hajjis," January 2005, at www.fco.gov.uk.

2. Zamzam water comes from a well near Kaaba, a cube-like structure believed to have been built by Abraham and his son. According to the Quran, when Ismail (the son of Abraham) and his mother Hagar were wandering in the desert searching for water, God sent the angel Gabriel to strike the earth. The waters that sprang forth are still drunk to this day and are believed to contain healing properties.

3. Wilhelm Heitmeyer, Joachim Muller, and Helmut Schroeder, *Verlockender Fundamentalismus: Turkische Jugendliche in Deutschland* (Frankfurt a.M.: Suhrkamp, 1997).

4. Timothy M. Savage, "Europe and Islam: Crescent Waxing, Cultures Clashing," *Washington Quarterly*, vol. 27, no. 3 (Summer 2004), pp. 25–50.

5. Tariq Ramadan, *To Be a European Muslim* (Leicester: Islamic Foundation Press, 1999).

6. Graham E. Fuller and Ian O. Lesser, *A Sense of Siege: The Geopolitics of Islam and the West* (Boulder, Colo.: Westview Press, 1995).

7. "O Father, Where Art Thou?" *Time International*, June 16, 2003.

8. Andrew Greeley, *Religion in Europe at the End of the Second Millennium* (New Brunswick, N.J.: Transaction, 2003).

Chapter 3. Two Faces, Two Futures

1. Cem Özdemir, *Ich bin Inlaender: Ein Anatolischer Schwabe im Bundestag* (Munich: Deutscher Taschenbuch Verlag, 1999), p. 16.

2. Patrick E. Tyler and Don Van Natta, Jr., "Militants in Europe Openly Call for Jihad and the Rule of Islam," *New York Times*, Apr. 26, 2004.

3. Stathis N. Kalyvas, "Unsecular Politics and Religious Mobilization: Beyond Christian Democracy," Thomas Kselman and Joseph A. Buttigieg,

eds., in *European Christian Democracy: Historical Legacies and Comparative Perspectives* (Notre Dame, Ind.: University of Notre Dame, 2003), p. 293.

Chapter 4. Headscarf Headaches, Cartoon Chaos

1. Jytte Klausen, "Rotten Judgment in the State of Denmark," Salon.com, Feb. 8, 2006.

2. "Manifesto: Together Facing the New Totalitarianism," *Jyllands-Posten*, Feb. 28, 2006.

3. Dan Bilefsky, "Danish Satirist, a Muslim, Sees Laughs Ebbing Away," *International Herald Tribune*, Feb. 5, 2006.

4. Merve Kavakçi, "Headscarf Heresy," *Foreign Policy*, May/June 2004, p. 66.

5. *Evening Mail*, Nov. 19, 2004.

6. Arlene MacLeod, *Accommodating Protest* (New York: Columbia University Press, 1991).

7. Alison Roberts, "I Won't Be Crying if I Lose: An Interview with Oona King," *Times of London*, Apr. 11, 2005.

8. Ernest Gellner, *Nations and Nationalism* (Oxford: Blackwell, 1983), p. 34.

9. Samira Bellil, *Dans l'enfer des Tournantes [In Gang Rape Hell]* (Paris: Denoël, 2003).

10. Christopher Dickey and Marie Valla, "Sexism in the Cities: Islamic Women in Paris Band Together against Abuse," *Newsweek International*, Aug. 18, 2003, p. 30.

11. Caitlin Killian, "The Other Side of the Veil: North African Women in France Respond to the Head Scarf Affair," *Gender and Society*, August 2003, pp. 567–90.

12. Associated Press, "German President Evaluates Headscarf Ban," *Seattle Post-Intelligencer*, Jan. 4, 2004.

13. Lorenzo Vidino and Erick Stakelbeck, "Along Came Sharia," *National Review Online*, Feb. 19, 2004.

14. Associated Press Worldstream, "French Court Issues Temporary Suspension Order for Deported Imam," Apr. 23, 2004.

15. Caroline Wheeler, "My Two Wives," *Sunday Mercury*, Dec. 14, 2003.

16. FGM is also practiced by some indigenous peoples in Colombia,

Mexico, and Peru. For more information on FGM, see the World Health Organization's fact sheet, www.who.int/mediacentre/factsheets/fs241/en/.

17. Zara Spencer, "The Criminalisation of Female Genital Mutilation in Queensland," *E Law, Murdoch University Electronic Journal of Law*, September 2002.

18. For an account of FGM among the Ethiopian Jews, see Asher Naim, *Saving the Lost Tribe: The Rescue and Redemption of the Ethiopian Jews* (New York: Ballantine, 2003).

Chapter 5. Migration Migraines

1. Behzad Yaghmaian, *Embracing the Infidel: Stories of Muslim Migrants on the Journey West* (New York: Delacorte Press, 2005). Roberto's story spans pages 76–89.

2. UNHCR, "Refugees by Numbers, 2005 Edition," www.unhcr.ch /cgi-bin/texis/vtx/basics/opendoc.htm?tbl=basics&id=3b028097c.

3. Nicola Smith, "Holland Launches the Immigrant Quiz," *Sunday Times*, Mar. 12, 2006.

4. "The Coming Demographic: How Aging Populations Will Reduce Global Savings," McKinsey and Co., January 2005, www.mckinsey.com.

5. The above statistics are drawn from a thorough, unclassified study compiled by the Strategic Assessments Group of the Office for Transnational Issues, Central Intelligence Agency.

6. Timothy M. Savage, "Europe and Islam: Crescent Waxing, Cultures Clashing," *Washington Quarterly*, vol. 27, no. 3 (Summer 2004), pp. 25–50.

7. "EU Commissioner Says Europe Needs Immigrants," *BBC Monitor*, Jan. 22, 2004.

8. Stephen Castles, *The Age of Migration: International Population Movements in the Modern World* (New York: Guilford Press, 1998).

9. Ibid., p. 15.

10. "Insular Japan Needs, but Resists, Immigration," *New York Times*, July 24, 2003.

11. Philip L. Martin, "Germany: Reluctant Land of Immigration," American Institute for Contemporary German Studies Policy Paper, 1998.

12. Philip Longman, *The Empty Cradle: How Falling Birthrates Threaten World Prosperity and What to Do about It* (New York: New America Books, 2004).

13. Jeremy Rifkin, *Hydrogen Economy: The Creation of the Worldwide Energy Web and the Redistribution of Power on Earth* (New York: J. P. Tarcher/Penguin, 2003).

14. Shireen Hunter, *Islam: Europe's Second Religion* (Washington, D.C.: Praeger, 2002).

15. A useful source on unemployment, poverty, and education statistics is compiled by the Muslim Council of Britain. See www.mcb.org.uk/mcbdirect/statistics.php.

16. Hunter, *Islam: Europe's Second Religion,* pp. 3–28.

17. Jocelyne Cesari, "Islam in the West: Modernity and Globalization Revisited," in Roy Mottahedeh, Birgit Schaebler, and Leif Stenberg, eds., *Globalization and the Muslim World: Culture, Religion, and Modernity* (Syracuse, N. Y.: Syracuse University Press, 2004). "Sociological analysis of Islam at the global level in a comparison with other religious systems will overcome the Orientalists' sharp and artificial contrast between Orient and Occident. It will demonstrate that world religions can actually accelerate the process of globalization by promoting shifts from communal to associative structures across nations. Religions will be shown not only to reinforce and recreate communal ties in response to globalization, but also to offer resources for new forms of individualization and modernization."

18. "Structuring Immigration, Fostering Integration," Report by the Independent Commission on Migration to Germany, Berlin, July 4, 2001, p. 1.

19. Pew Global Attitudes Project 2005, June 23, 2005, at www.pewglobal.org.

20. Stefan Luft, *Mechanismen, Manipulation, Missbrauch: Ausländerpolitik und Ausländerintegration in Deutschland* (Cologne: Verlag Wissenschaft und Politik, 2002), pp. 99–126. Luft reports that 40% of foreigners admit that they do not speak good German, only 34% said they speak primarily in German every day, and only 20% of Turkish immigrants speak mostly German on a day-to-day basis. In 1997, only 19.4% of foreigners completed their secondary education (p. 102). Luft details criminal statistics (pp. 104–5), showing the high percentage of crimes committed by foreigners relative to foreigners' percent of the total population. He also shows that from 1984 to 1997 in West Germany, violent crimes committed by those aged 14–20 tripled, two-thirds of which were perpetrated

by foreigners (p. 113). A 1998 study of youth crime conducted by Lower Saxony's Justice Minister concluded that crime is lower where foreigners are better integrated (p. 114). Most federal statistics do not use religion as a category. It is therefore unclear precisely what percentage of these statistics on foreigners Muslims comprise.

21. "Kulturell-Religioese Einstellungen und Soziooekonomisch Lage junger turkischer Migranten in der Bundesrepublik," June 2000. Polls performed by the Deutsch-Turkisch Studien in Essen, under the direction of Gulay Kizilocak. The authors surveyed 2,014 Turkish Muslims.

22. Timothy Garton Ash, *The Guardian*, Aug. 14, 2003.

Chapter 6. Clash of the Barbies

1. AP, "Saudi Religious Police Say Barbie Is a Moral Threat," www.foxnews.com, Sept. 10, 2003.

2. "Globalization and Gender Relations in Iran: The Challenge from Barbie and Ken," www.msu.edu/user/hillrr/161lec28.htm, accessed May 4, 2004.

3. Once again, boys are given better odds of success. Their chances of being shaped like Ken are estimated at 1 in 50. "Fascinating Facts about the Invention of the Barbie® Doll by Ruth Handler in 1959," www.ideafinder.com/history/inventions/story081.htm, accessed Apr. 11, 2004.

4. For more on how America's religious landscape has been steadily transforming, and particularly for a description of the mosques and Buddhist and Hindu temples to be found in large and small towns across the U.S., see Diana L. Eck, *A New Religious America: How a "Christian Country" Has Now Become the World's Most Religiously Diverse Nation* (San Francisco: HarperCollins, 2002).

5. Eric Pfanner, "Concern about U.S. Foreign Policy Has Some Reevaluating Ad Tactics," *New York Times*, Jan. 20, 2004.

6. John A. Quelch, as interviewed by Sean Silverthorne, "Will American Brands Be a Casualty of War?" Harvard Business School *Working Knowledge*, http://hbswk.hbs.edu/item.jhtml?id=3429&t=marketing.

7. John A. Quelch and Douglas B. Holt, "The Post-9/11 Resilience of American Brands," *Strategy and Business* 34 (Spring 2004), pp. 8–10.

8. Craig S. Smith, "The Market McDonald's Missed: The Muslim Burger," *New York Times*, Sept. 16, 2005.

9. See Mecca Cola's website, http://www.mecca-cola.com/en/presskit
.php.

10. Osama bin Laden, *The Observer*, Nov. 24, 2002.

11. Yossef Bodansky, *Bin Laden: The Man Who Declared War on America*
(New York: Crown, 2001), Ch. 2.

12. "Boycotting Israeli and American Goods," IslamOnline, Apr. 18,
2004, at www.islamonline.net.

13. "Boycotting Products of the US and Its Allies: Obligatory?" IslamOnline, Mar. 22, 2003, at www.islamonline.net.

14. IslamicAwakening.com, "Call to Boycott All Zionist-Supporting
Companies in the World," www.islamicawakening.com.

15. Caravan Saray (now Zaid's), http://store.yahoo.net/caravansaray
/info-our-mission.html.

16. Meat and Livestock Commission press release, October 2001, on
"Muslim Lamb Campaign."

17. "As Al Safa Grows So Does Opposition to It," www.SoundVision
.com.

18. DataMonitor, 2004.

19. "British Muslim Students Seek '*Halal* Loans,'" *The Guardian*, Apr.
26, 2003.

20. See www.Islamiqmoney.com.

21. "British Muslim Students Seek '*Halal* Loans.'"

22. Shariffa Carlo, IslamicAwakening.com, "Muslims Wake Up!"
www.islamicawakening.com.

Chapter 7. New Europe, Same Old Issues

1. "Praying for a Mosque," *Slovenia News* (Ministry of Foreign Affairs),
Dec. 16, 2003, at www.slonews.sta.si.

Chapter 8. The Future of Muslim Europe

1. An aspect of this fictional account was inspired by Beverly Crawford,
"Die Lady Bismarck leidet," *Cicero*, October 2004, pp. 58–63.

2. For a detailed account of Grover Norquist, see John Cassidy, "The
Ringleader," *The New Yorker*, Aug. 1, 2005, pp. 42–53.

3. Grover Norquist, "The New Fifth Column," American Enterprise
Institute, June 1, 2003.

Conclusion. Looking Back to Look Ahead

1. John McGreevy, *Catholicism and American Freedom: A History* (New York: W. W. Norton, 2003), particularly the introduction and chapter 1.

2. Ibid., p. 131.

3. François Duchêne, *Jean Monnet: The First Statesman of Interdependence* (New York: W. W. Norton, 1994), p. 13.

Epilogue. Attracting the Second Circle

1. William Bennett, "Remembering Why We Fight," www.claremont.org/writings/040519bennett.html, accessed Sept. 15, 2004.

2. National Public Radio, *Talk of the Nation*, Aug. 26, 2004.

3. "U.S. Senator Richard Lugar (R-IN) Holds a Hearing on the Nomination of Condoleezza Rice to be Secretary of State," *Congressional Quarterly*, Jan. 18, 2005.

4. Peter W. Singer, "Six Guidelines to Improve American Public Diplomacy" (op-ed), *The Daily Star*, Feb. 28, 2004, www.brookings.edu.

5. Patricia Harrison Testimony to the House International Relations Committee, http://usinfo.state.gov/mena/Archive/2004/Aug/19-981349 .html.

6. Michael Scheuer, *Imperial Hubris: Why the West Is Losing the War on Terror* (Washington, D.C.: Brassey's, 2004).

7. Joseph Stiglitz, *Globalization and Its Discontents* (New York: W. W. Norton, 2003).

8. Amanda Paulson and Sara B. Miller, "More Grist for Campaigns: Poverty in America Rises," *Christian Science Monitor*, Aug. 27, 2004. See also "Pay: Winners and Losers," *The Economist*, May 8, 1999, pp. 5–8.

9. Jimmy Carter, *Our Endangered Values: America's Moral Crisis* (New York: Simon & Schuster, 2005), pp. 192–93.

10. "Jerry Falwell Calls Islam's Prophet a 'Terrorist,'" *Turkish Times*, Oct. 15–31, 2002. See also Todd Hertz, "Riots, Condemnation, Fatwa, and Apology Follow Falwell's CBS Comments," *Christianity Today*, Oct. 14, 2002.

11. Ayub Khan, "Reverend Jerry Falwell and His Anti-Muslim Rant," IslamOnline, March 3, 2001, www.islamonline.net/english /Politics/2001/03/article9.shtml, accessed Sept. 9, 2005.

12. *Spiritual Perspectives on America's Role as a Superpower* (Woodstock, Vt.: Skylight Paths, 2003), p. 66.

13. Ibid., p. 67.

14. Ibid., p. 73.

15. In a thought-provoking study, *Metaphors We Live By* (Chicago: University of Chicago Press, 2003 [1980]), linguists George Lakoff and Mark Johnson showed how metaphors profoundly affect the way people think and the damage they can cause.

16. Emanuel Adler and Beverly Crawford, "Constructing a Mediterranean Region: A Cultural Approach," paper presented at the Conference on "The Convergence of Civilizations? Constructing a Mediterranean Region," Arrábida Monastery, Fundação Oriente, Lisboa, Portugal, June 6–9, 2002.

17. Carter, *Our Endangered Values*, p. 121.

18. For a firsthand account of the origins of the OSS and the Research and Analysis Branch, see William L. Langer, *In and Out of the Ivory Tower: The Autobiography of William L. Langer* (New York: Neale Watson Academic Publications, 1977).

Bibliography

Abul al-Mawdudi, Sayyid. *Towards Understanding Islam*. Leicester: Islamic Foundation, 1981.

AlSayyad, Nezar, and Manuel Castells, eds. *Muslim Europe or Euro-Islam: Politics, Culture, and Citizenship in the Age of Globalization*. Lanham, Md.: Lexington Books, 2002. Co-published with the Center for Middle Eastern Studies. Berkeley: University of California.

Benhabib, Seyla. *The Claims of Culture: Equality and Diversity in the Global Era*. Princeton: Princeton University Press, 2002.

Bistolfi, Robert, and François Zabbal. *Islams d'Europe: intégration ou insertion communautaire?* (Islam in Europe: Integration or Communitarian Insertion?) Paris: Editions de l'Aube, 1995.

Bodansky, Yossef. *Bin Laden: The Man Who Declared War on America*. New York: Crown Publishing Group, 2001.

Brubaker, Rogers. *Immigration and the Politics of Citizenship in Europe and North America*. Lanham, Md.: University Press of America; [Washington, D.C.]: German Marshall Fund of the United States, 1989.

———. *Nationalism Reframed: Nationhood and the National Question in the New Europe*. Cambridge, England, and New York: Cambridge University Press, 1996.

———. *National Minorities, Nationalizing States, and External National Homelands in the New Europe: Notes toward a Relational Analysis*. Vienna: Institut für Höhere Studien, 1993.

———. *Citizenship and Nationhood in France and Germany*. Cambridge, Mass.: Harvard University Press, 1992.

Carter, Jimmy. *Our Endangered Values: America's Moral Crisis*. New York: Simon & Schuster, 2005.

Castles, Stephen. *The Age of Migration: International Population Movements in the Modern World.* New York: Guilford Press, 1998.

Cesari, Jocelyne. "Islam in the West: Modernity and Globalization Revisited," in Roy Mottahedeh, Birgit Schaebler, and Leif Stenberg, eds., *Globalization and the Muslim World: Culture, Religion, and Modernity.* Syracuse, N.Y.: Syracuse University Press, 2004.

———. *When Islam and Democracy Meet: Muslims in Europe and in the United States.* New York: Palgrave Macmillan, 2004.

Cowles, Maria Green, James Caporaso, and Thomas Risse, eds. *Transforming Europe: Europeanization and Domestic Change.* Ithaca, N.Y.: Cornell University Press, 2001.

Dassetto, Felice. *La construction de l'Islam européen: approche socio-anthropologique* (The Construction of European Islam: A Socio-Anthropological Approach). Paris: l'Harmattan, 1996.

Esposito, John L. *Islam and Politics.* Syracuse, N.Y.: Syracuse University Press, 1998.

———, and John O. Voll. *Islam and Democracy.* New York: Oxford University Press, 1996.

Ferrari, Silvio, ed. *L'Islam in Europa: lo statuto giuridico della communità musulmane* (Islam in Europe: The Juridical Status of Muslim Communities in Europe). Bolognà: il Mulino, 1996.

Fuller, Graham E., and Ian O. Lesser. *A Sense of Siege: The Geopolitics of Islam and the West.* Boulder, Colo.: Westview, 1995.

Gellner, Ernest. *Nations and Nationalism.* Oxford: Blackwell, 1983.

Greeley, Andrew. *Religion in Europe at the End of the Second Millennium.* New Brunswick, N.J.: Transaction Publishers, 2003.

Gutmann, Amy, ed. *Multiculturalism: Examining the Politics of Recognition.* Princeton: Princeton University Press, 1994.

Heitmeyer, Wilhelm, Joachim Muller, and Helmut Schroeder, *Verlockender Fundamentalismus: Turkische Jugendliche in Deutschland.* Frankfurt a.M.: Suhrkamp, 1997.

Hunter, Shireen T. *The Future of Islam and the West: Clash of Civilizations or Peaceful Coexistence?* Westport, Conn.: Praeger, 1998.

———. *Islam, Europe's Second Religion: The New Social, Cultural, and Political Landscape.* Westport, Conn.: Praeger, 2002.

———, ed. *The Politics of Islamic Revivalism: Diversity and Unity.* Bloomington, Ind.: Indiana University Press, 1988.

Jacobson, J. *Islam in Transition: Religion and Identity among British Pakistani Youth*. London, Routledge, 1998.

Joly, Daniele. *Britain's Crescent: Making a Place for Islam in British Society*. Aldershot: Avebury, 1995.

Kalyvas, Stathis N. "Unsecular Politics and Religious Mobilization: Beyond Christian Democracy," in Thomas Kselman and Joseph A. Buttigieg, eds., *European Christian Democracy: Historical Legacies and Comparative Perspectives*. Notre Dame: University of Notre Dame Press, 2003.

Kepel, Gilles. *Jihad: The Trail of Political Islam*. Cambridge, Mass.: Harvard University Press, 2002.

———. *Les banlieves de l'Islam* (The Suburbs of Islam). Paris: Seuil, 1987.

———. *The War for Muslim Minds: Islam and the West*. Cambridge, Mass.: Harvard University Press, 2004.

Khosrokhavar, F. *Islam des jeunes* (Islam of the Youth). Paris: Flammarion, 1997.

Klausen, Jytte. *The Islamic Challenge: Politics and Religion in Western Europe*. New York: Oxford University Press, 2005.

Lewis, Bernard. *What Went Wrong: Western Impact and Middle Eastern Response*. New York: Oxford University Press, 2002.

Lewis, Philip. *Islamic Britain: Religion, Politics, and Identity among British Muslims*. London: Tauris, 1994.

Longman, Philip. *The Empty Cradle: How Falling Birthrates Threaten World Prosperity and What to Do about It*. New York: New America Books, 2004.

Luft, Stefan. *Mechanismen, Manipulation, Missbrauch: Ausländerpolitik und Ausländerintegration in Deutschland*. Koeln: Verlag Wissenschaft und Politik, 2002.

McGreevy, John. *Catholicism and American Freedom: A History*. New York: W. W. Norton, 2003.

Metcalf, Barbara Daly, ed. *Making Muslim Space in North America and Europe*. Berkeley: University of California Press, 1996.

Nielsen, Jorgen. *Muslims in Western Europe*. Edinburgh: Edinburgh University Press, 1995.

Nonneman, Gerd, Tim Niblock, and Bogdan Szajkowski. *Muslim Communities in the New Europe*. Reading: Ithaca Press, 1996.

Özdemir, Cem. *Ich bin Inlaender: Ein Anatolischer Schwabe im Bundestag.* Munich: Deutscher Taschenbuch Verlag, 1999.

Pape, Robert. *Dying to Win: The Strategic Logic of Suicide Terrorism.* New York: Random House, 2005.

Ramadan, Tariq. *To Be a European Muslim.* Leicester: Islamic Foundation Press, 1999.

Rex, John, and Robert Moore. *Race, Community and Conflict.* Oxford: Oxford University Press, 1967.

Rifkin, Jeremy. *Hydrogen Economy: The Creation of the Worldwide Energy Web and the Redistribution of Power on Earth.* New York: J. P. Tarcher/Penguin, 2003.

Roy, Olivier. *The Failure of Political Islam.* Cambridge, Mass.: Harvard University Press, 1994.

———. *Globalized Islam: The Search for a New Ummah.* New York: Columbia University Press, 2004.

Shadid, W. A. R., and P. S. van Koningsveld, eds. *Muslims in the Margin: Political Responses to the Presence of Islam in Western Europe.* Kampen: Kok Pharos, 1996.

———. *Religious Freedom and the Position of Islam in Western Europe.* Kampen: Kok Pharos, 1995.

Spuler-Stegemann. *Muslime in Deutschland: Nebeneinander oder Miteinander.* Freiburg: Herder, 1998.

Tibi, Bassam. *Islam between Culture and Politics.* Hampshire, U.K.: Palgrave, 2001.

Yaghmaian, Behzad. *Embracing the Infidel: Stories of Muslim Migrants on the Journey West.* New York: Delacorte, 2005.

Index